ILLUMINATI

AGENDA 21

The Luciferian Plan To Destroy Creation

Dean and Jill Henderson

© 2018 Dean Henderson and Jill Henderson

Cover and interior design by Jill Henderson

ISBN-10: 1720819106
ISBN-13: 978-1720819103

DEDICATION

To Mother Earth and To Humanity
We Are One

CONTENTS

CHAPTER 1

LEAVING THE GARDEN OF EDEN

In the Book of Genesis Adam and Eve - certainly a metaphor for humanity - landed in the Garden of Eden, a paradise of abundance that only required the acceptance, contentment and gratitude of the humans to remain intact and fertile.

Despite God's warning and tempted by the serpent - a metaphor for Lucifer and the Anunnaki, whose Nephilim hybrid offspring are also mentioned in the Book of Genesis - the first humans ate the apple from the tree of knowledge and were cast out of the Garden of Eden.

Rather than being content with being human, with seeing themselves as connected to the entirety of God's creation, Adam and Eve began a process of intellectual self-worship, which today has supplanted all holy books to become the religion of the emerging Luciferian New World Order.

As humanity was forced away from nature by an emerging Babylonian priesthood of Satanists - first, via agriculture as per the story of Cain and Abel and later, via industrialization and capitalism - we lost our God-given abilities to heal ourselves, create free energy, find food in Creator's wild garden and connect telepathically with other beings.

We went from having seven senses to believing we only have five. We were intentionally crippled by the Luciferians. We fell out of love with Mother Earth.

The universe is 93% energy and 7% matter. With this understanding we should remember the Lakota saying, "We are not much, but we are a whole lot more than nothing". Our bodies are just a shell containing our soul, our vital energy, which is free in the knowledge that we are all actually One.

A priesthood of secret societies emerged who were obsessed with the Luciferian idea that man is smarter than the Creator. They prided themselves on being fallen angels. The ancient cities of Ur and Babylon were ruled by these Luciferians, who justified their deceptions using evil texts like the Talmud and Cabala. They eventually coalesced around the pyramids of Giza, enslaving the Israelites to cover up the real reason that ancient people - probably black African Moors - built the pyramids.

As researcher Michael Tellinger and others are finding out, the pyramids were an important part of a free energy grid spanning the planet, a grid that includes all the ancient ruins from Machu Picchu to Angkor Wat to Ayers Rock. From the air, many of these ruins look like computer circuit boards. It's all about silicon and water. Human beings are 75% water and if tuned in, are excellent conductors.

The Luciferian brain worshipers literally covered up this fact by topping-off the structures, then from their Grand Lodge of Cairo headquarters, created an Egyptian Triad as a template for the establishment of a pyramid-shaped economic, social and religious system that they have used to enslave the rest of humanity.

They called themselves the Brotherhood of the Snake, again a metaphor for the snake that tempted humanity away from their hunting and gathering existence in the Garden of Eden.

In fact, these Luciferians looted and pillaged all the wealth and resources from this Garden of Eden, and usurped the ancient wisdom. They then hid this wisdom from the masses and slaughtered aboriginal people around the globe who *were* content in the garden and lived harmoniously in the knowledge that they were just a part of God's creation.

They stole the seven-sense knowledge of the indigenous people and hid it from humanity within their secret societies where they lorded over it and called it the Ancient Mysteries, though there was nothing mysterious about it. It was simply reality.

The Luciferian philosophy is one of division, individualism, conquest and the atomization of the whole. They reject the reality of nature, which is that we are all One.

Where the ancient ones knew that Mother Earth was a whole living breathing organism called Gaia, the worshipers of the fallen angel saw it as a resource to be owned and plundered for personal financial gain. Materialism is the their religion.

As their wealth has accumulated, so has their bad karma. Instead of facing it, they remain in denial and burrow deeper into their Luciferian delusion as to the nature of reality.

As a result of this lack of understanding of the nature of reality, they live in ignorance and bondage. And so they work tirelessly to make sure we also dwell in this same fourth dimension of bondage, chasing money and fame instead of embracing reality and being happy.

The New Science renaissance being led by quantum physics is exposing the lies that these physical, intellectual and emotional hoarder pirates have enslaved us in, proving that science itself has a spiritual, rather than an objectified basis.

The Luciferians know this, so an epic battle between Good and Evil is entering a critical phase. While truth lies in unity and wholeness, they seek to divide, disrupt and obfuscate.

Whether their deliberate attempt to destroy humanity and this planet is a result of sheer ignorance, or terraforming for a coming return of their Anunnaki lizard cousins doesn't really matter.

These most misguided, miserable and dense humans on the planet - these baby sacrificing, depopulation-obsessed war-mongering vampire inbreds - are so deranged that they think they are smarter than us. Thus, they pompously call themselves the Illuminati.

PART I

THE LUCIFERIAN PERPETRATORS

CHAPTER 2

THE ROTHSCHILD ILLUMINATI

While the Luciferians hide in the shadows and try to manipulate creation, it is tactically important that they be identified and become household names. These delusional psychopaths have declared war on humanity and if we are to survive as a species, we who are One must now take the fight to them by exposing their agenda.

Once a critical mass of awareness is reached, the Satanists will melt away into the shadows. But to reach that awareness we need to know who they are, how they think and what they have planned.

The Illuminati serves as ruling council to all the Luciferian secret societies. Its roots go back to the Guardians of Light in Atlantis, the Brotherhood of the Snake in Sumeria, the Afghan Roshaniya, the Egyptian Mystery Schools and the Genoese families who bankrolled the Roman Empire and hung Jesus Christ on the cross for exposing them.

British Prime Minister Benjamin Disraeli, who "handled" mafia-founder and 33rd Degree Mason, Giuseppe Mazzini, alluded to the Illuminati in a daring speech before the House of Commons in 1856 warning, "There is in Italy a power which we seldom mention. I mean the secret societies. Europe is covered with a network of secret societies just as the surfaces of the earth are covered with a network of railroads."

The Illuminati is to these secret societies what the Bank of International Settlements is to the Eight Families central bankers. Their hierarchy consists of exactly the same people. The forerunners of the Freemasons - the Knights Templar - founded the concept of banking and created a "bond market" as a means to control European nobles through war debts.

The Templars claim to possess secret knowledge that Jesus Christ married Mary Magdalene, fathered children and was the son of Joseph of Arimathea. This is a lie based on the fact that Joseph was the son of King Solomon. Solomon's Temple thus became the model for Masonic Temples, which are found without fail in every town of any size in America.

The Freemasons are officially Crown Agents who work to further the Satanic goals of world domination hatched by the City of London and the Bank of International Settlements crowd.

Solomon's Temple was a place of ill repute where fornicating, drunkenness and human sacrifice were the norm. These Babylonians justified these deeds based on the Luciferian Talmud. Its location on Jerusalem's Mount Moriah may have also been an Anunnaki flight control center.

The Crusader Knights Templar looted a huge store of gold and numerous sacred artifacts from beneath the Temple, which they used to found the Holy Roman Empire. King Solomon was the son of King David who, during his 1015 BC reign, massacred thousands of people. This claimed-lineage to the House of David is what the Illuminati use to justify their global control.

Author David Icke calls King David "a butcher" and asserts that the king wrote a good chunk of the Bible. His son Solomon killed his own brother to become King. He advised the Egyptian Pharaoh Shishak and married his daughter. Solomon studied at Akhenaten's Egyptian Mystery Schools, where mind control was rampant. The Grand Lodge of Cairo spawned both the Assassins and the terrorist Afghan Roshaniya. Solomon returned to Jerusalem to build his Temple with help from Egyptian Brotherhood brick Freemasons.

The Canaanite Brotherhood was headed by the god-king Melchizedek, who may have been an Anunnaki. The king focused on a Hebrew understanding of the Ancient Mysteries. The Order of Melchizedek became the secret society associated with the Cabala. King Solomon developed his vast wisdom studying the Sumerian Tablets of Destiny, which Abraham possessed.

Abraham may have also been of Anunnaki origin. Both he and Melchizedek had been tutored by the Sumerian Brotherhood of the Snake, represented in the Biblical creation story when Adam and Eve are tempted from the bountiful garden of Eden (a hunting and gathering existence) into a world of "sin and servitude" by a snake. Eve could have also been impregnated by the snake - an Anunnaki serpent - thus damning all Adamus (the Sumerian word for human beings) to a life of toil under serpent king bloodline control.

The basis of the Sumerian Tablets of Destiny that Abraham possessed were known as *Ha Qabala*, Hebrew for "light and knowledge". Those who understood these cryptic secrets believed to be encoded throughout the Old Testament, are referred to deferentially as *Ram*. The phrase is used in Celtic, Buddhist and Hindu spiritual circles as well. The Knights Templar brought Cabalistic knowledge to Europe when they returned from their Middle East Crusade adventures.

The Knights created the Prieuré de Sion on Mt. Zion near Jerusalem in the 11th century to guard such holy relics as the Shroud of Turin, the Ark of the Covenant, and the Hapsburg family's Spear of Destiny, which was used to kill Jesus Christ.

The Priory's more important purpose was to guard Templar gold and to preserve the alleged bloodline of Jesus - the royal Sangreal - which they believe is carried forth by the French Bourbon Merovingian family and the related Hapsburg monarchs of Spain and Austria. The French Lorraine dynasty, which descended from the Merovingians, married into the House of Hapsburg to acquire the throne of Austria.

The Hapsburgs ran the Holy Roman Empire until its dissolution in 1806 through King Charles V and others. The family traces its roots back to a Swiss estate known as Habichtsburg, which was built in 1020. The Hapsburgs are an integral part of the Priory of Sion. Many researchers are convinced that Spain's Hapsburg King Philip will be crowned Sangreal World King in Jerusalem.

The Hapsburgs are related to the Rothschilds through the Holy Roman Emperor, Frederick Barbarossa's second son, Archibald II. The Rothschilds - leaders in Cabala, Freemasonry and the Knights Templar - sit at the apex of the both the Illuminati and the Eight Families banking cartel. The family accumulated its vast wealth by issuing war bonds to the Black Nobility for centuries, including the British Windsors, the French Bourbons, the German von Thurn und Taxis, the Italian Savoys and the Austrian and Spanish Hapsburgs.

David Icke believes the Rothschilds represent the head of the Anunnaki Serpent Kings, stating, "They (Rothschilds) had the crown heads of Europe in debt to them and this included the Black Nobility dynasty, the Hapsburgs, who ruled the Holy Roman Empire for 600 years. The Rothschilds also control the Bank of England. If there was a war, the Rothschilds were behind the scenes, creating conflict and funding both sides."

The Rothschilds and the Warburgs - who funded both Hitler and the Bolsheviks - are main stockholders of the German Bundesbank. The Rothschilds control Japan's biggest banking house, Nomura Securities, via a tie-up between Edmund Rothschild and Tsunao Okumura. The Rothschilds are the richest and most powerful family in the world. Their wealth is hidden by City of London-created off-shore accounts that show no ownership. The only one who knows who controls these accounts is the Bank of England, which the Rothschilds also control. They are also inbred. Over half of the last generation of Rothschild progeny married within the family, presumably to preserve their "Sangreal".

The 1782 Great Seal of the United States is loaded with Illuminati symbolism. So is the reverse side of the US $1 Federal Reserve Note, which was designed by Freemasons. The pyramid on the left side is derived from those in Egypt - a possible space beacon or energy source for the Anunnaki - whose Pharaohs oversaw the building of the pyramids using Israelite slave labor.

The pyramid is an important symbol for the Illuminati bankers. They call themselves Illuminati because there are 33 vertebrae in the human back. The highest level of Masonry is the 33rd Degree. Above that are the Illuminati, who believe they are the head sitting above the vertebrae, thus giving them the right to herd humanity in whatever direction they see fit - the ultimate expression of the Luciferian doctrine.

Thus, the Illuminati employ Triads, Trilaterals and Trinities to create a society ruled by the few elite Sangreal presiding over the masses, which is represented by the pyramid. When the Brotherhood of the Snake occupied the Grand Lodge of Cairo they worshiped a trinity of Isis, Osiris, and Horus, who may have been Anunnaki offspring.

The Brotherhood spread the concept of trinity to the Christian (Father, Son and Holy Spirit), Hindu (Brahma, Shiva and Krishna), and Buddhist (Buddha, Dharma and Sangha) faiths.

The eye atop the pyramid depicted on the $1 bill is the all-seeing eye of the Afghan Roshaniya, known alternately as The Order, and the Order of the Quest - names later adopted by Skull and Bones, Germanenorden, and the JASON Society.

Novus Ordo Seclorum appears beneath the pyramid, while *Annuit Coeptis* appears above the all-seeing eye. *Annuit Coeptis* means "may he smile upon our endeavors (Great Work of Ages)".

Above the eagle on the right side of the note are the words *E Pluribus Unum*, Latin for "out of many one". The eagle clutches 13 arrows and 13 olive branches while 13 stars appear above the eagle's head. America was founded with 13 "colonies". Templar pirate Jacques de Molay was executed on Friday the 13th.

The numbers 3, 9, 13, and 33 are significant to the secret societies. The Bilderberger Group has a powerful Policy Committee of 13 members. It is one of 3 committees of 13 that answer to Prince Bernhard - a member of the Hapsburg family and leader of the Black Nobility. The Bilderberg Policy Committee answers to a Rothschild Round Table of 9.

The ancient spiritual texts tell us that numbers are the basis of creation, so these same numbers are key to understanding reality.

But again, the Luciferians have hijacked this spiritual knowledge, hidden it from us with their secret societies, inverted it and used it to reinforce their fourth-dimension madness.

One of the goals of the Illuminati's Freemason lieutenants is to study the holy texts in order to glean information that can be inverted and deployed to advance their sociopathic agenda.

As Jamaican revolutionary reggae artist Peter Tosh said of these Babylonians, "Everything you do upside down".

CHAPTER 3

PROTOCOLS OF THE ELDERS OF ZION

The current worldwide Crown reign of terror on behalf of the banker elite is reminiscent of a blueprint for global domination that first emerged in the mid-1800's. The document, known as the Protocols of the Wise Men of Zion, was obtained by the daughter of a Russian general after she paid a bribe of 2,500 French francs to a member of the Mizraim Freemason Lodge in Paris, which is home to the inner circle of the Knights Templar known as the Priory of Sion.

The Priory of Sion elite believe that Jesus faked his death with the help of certain herbs, then married the administer of those herbs, Mary Magdalene. The Priory believes the couple fled to southern France and had numerous children. During the 5th century, the theory goes, Jesus' descendants married into the Frank royalty from which France takes its name, thus creating the Merovingian Dynasty. This royal blood or Sangreal is the justification the Crown uses to legitimize its rule over humanity.

By the 13th century, the Knights Templars used their looted gold to buy 9,000 castles throughout Europe from which they ran an empire stretching from Copenhagen to Damascus. It was the wealth used to establish the Roman Empire.

The robber baron Templars founded modern banking techniques and legitimized usury - also known as interest payments. Templar banks popped up everywhere, backed by their newfound gold wealth. They charged up to 60% interest on loans, launched the concepts of trust accounts and bond markets, and introduced a credit card system for Holy Land pilgrims. They acted as tax collectors, though they themselves were exempted by Roman authorities. And having also found instructions regarding secret building techniques under Solomon's Temple, the Templars built the great cathedrals of Europe. The stained glass used in these cathedrals resulted from a secret Gothic technique known by few. One who had perfected this art was Omar Khayyam, a good friend of Assassin-founder Hasan bin Sabah.

The Templars controlled a huge fleet of ships and their own naval fleet based at the French Atlantic Port of La Rochelle. They were first to use magnetic compasses for navigation and were especially cozy with the royals of England. They purchased the island of Cyprus from Richard the Lion Heart, but were later overrun by the Turks.

On Friday October 13, 1307, King Philip IV of France joined forces with Pope Clement V and began rounding up Templars on charges ranging from necromancy to the use of black magic. Friday the 13th would, from that day forward, carry negative connotations. It was then that the Templars packed up their loot, signed onto the Magna Carta and established their current lair in the Freemason City of London.

"Sion" is believed to be a transliteration of Zion, itself a transliteration for the ancient Hebrew name "Jerusalem". The Priory of Sion first came into public view in July 1956. A 1981 notice in the French press listed 121 dignitaries as Priory members. All were bankers, royalty or members of the international political jet set. Pierre Plantard was listed as Grand Master.

Plantard is a direct descendant, through King Dagobert II, of the Merovingian Kings. Plantard, who owns property in the Rennes-le-

Chateau area of southern France where the Priory of Sion is based, has stated that the order has in its possession lost treasure recovered from beneath Solomon's Temple and that it will be returned to Israel when the time is right. He also stated that in the near future monarchy would be restored to France and other nations.

The Protocols of the Wise Men of Zion was first published in an 1864 French book, Dialogue in Hell Between Machiavelli and Montesquieu or the Politics of Machiavelli in the Nineteenth Century by a Contemporary. By the 1890's Russian Professor Sergei Nilus had published the Protocols in his book, The Great Within the Small: The Coming Anti-Christ. Nilus was arrested and tortured and the Protocols were suppressed for many more decades. The Protocols were a manifesto written by a secret society that claimed itself superior to the rest of mankind, using the Hebrew word *goyim* (cattle) to refer to the masses.

Anti-Semites, including Hitler, have used the Protocols to falsely attack "a Jewish conspiracy". But the Protocols authors were not Jewish. Rather, they were Satanists intent on creating a political movement called Zionism, which seeks to use Israel as its linchpin for City of London global hegemony and as guardian of the vast Rothschild/Rockefeller oil reserves of the Middle East region.

The movement is spearheaded by Illuminati Satanist secret societies such as the Knights Templar, Freemasons, Cabala and Muslim Brotherhood. Its power center has moved from Sumeria to Egypt to Rome and is now in the City of London - a one square mile separate jurisdiction within, but not governed by, London or the United Kingdom. The Illuminati nucleus of this movement is Luciferian in orientation. What follows are excerpts from the Protocols of the Wise Men of Zion:

Protocol 4: "In order to give the goyim no time to think and take note, their minds must be diverted towards industry and trade. Thus, all nations will be swallowed up in the pursuit of gain and...will not take note of their common foe. But, again, in order that freedom may once and for all disintegrate and ruin the communities of goyim, we must put industry on a speculative basis, the result of which will be that what is withdrawn from the land by industry will slip through their hands and pass into speculation, that is, to our classes."

Protocol 10: "It is from us that all-engulfing terror proceeds. We have in our service persons of all opinions: monarchists, demagogues, socialists trying to overthrow all established authority. By these acts all states are in torture; they exhort tranquility, are ready to sacrifice anything for peace. But we don't give them peace until they openly acknowledge our international super-government, and with submissiveness to utterly exhaust humanity with dissension, hatred, struggle, envy and even by use of torture, by starvation, by inoculation of diseases, by want, so that the goyim see no other issue than to take refuge in our complete sovereignty in money."

Protocol 13: "And how far-seeing were our learned elders when they said that to attain a serious goal behooves not to stop at any means or to count the victims sacrificed. We have not counted the victims of the goy cattle. In order that the masses themselves may not guess what they are about we must further distract them with amusements, games, pastimes, passions, people's palaces...these interests will finally distract them from questions in which we should find ourselves compelled to oppose them. Growing more and more unaccustomed to reflect and form opinions of their own, people will begin to talk in the same tone as we, because we alone shall be offering them new directions of thought."

Protocol 15: "We shall create and multiply Freemasonic Lodges in all countries of the world, absorb into them all who may become or who are prominent in public activity, for in these Lodges we shall find our principle intelligence office and means of influence. Among the members of these Lodges will be almost all the agents of international and national police since their service is for us irreplaceable in the respect that the police are in a position not only to use its own particular measures with the insubordinate, but also to screen our activities and provide pretexts and disguises. All these Lodges we shall bring under one central administration, known only to us and to all others absolutely unknown, which will be composed of our learned elders (Illuminati). The most secret political plots will be known to us and will fall under our guiding hands on the very day of their conception."

Protocol 16: "...we shall emasculate the first stage of collectivism - the universities...any form of study of ancient history...we shall replace with the study of the program of the future. We shall erase from the memory of men all facts of previous centuries which are undesirable for us. Each...life must be trained within strict limits corresponding to its destination and work in life. The system of bridling thought is already at work in the so-called system of teaching by object lessons (objectivity). In our program one-third of our subjects will keep the rest under observation. It will be no disgrace to be a spy".

Another section of the Protocols states, "We are the chosen, we are the only true men. Our minds give off the true power of the spirit; the intelligence of the rest of the world is merely instinctive and animal. They can see, but they cannot foresee. Does it not follow that nature herself has predestined us to dominate the world. Outwardly we (will) do our best to appear honorable and cooperative. A statesman's words do not have to agree with his acts. If we pursue these principles, the governments and peoples which we have thus prepared will take our IOU's for cash...the substitution of interest-bearing money... Economic crises have been produced by us...by no other means than the withdrawal of money from circulation... One day they will accept us as benefactors and saviors of the human race. If any state dared to resist us, if its neighbors make common cause with it against us, we will unleash global war."

Though decried as a forgery by the Illuminati propaganda networks of mainstream media, the Protocols of the Wise Men of Zion have been taken seriously by many scholars, along with political and economic leaders including Germany's Kaiser Wilhelm II, Russia's Czar Nicholas II and American industrialist Henry Ford.

The document refers often to the "ancient mysteries", the "seed of David" and the "symbolic snake". Its concluding statement reads, "Signed by the representatives of Sion of the 33rd Degree."

CHAPTER 4

DIRTY MONEY & THE ANUNNAKI

All of the "ancient mysteries" guarded by the Illuminati secret societies played out in Sumeria along the banks of the Tigris and Euphrates Rivers in Mesopotamia, where Sumerian clay tablets say man was forced into agriculture from a Garden of Eden hunter gatherer existence by Anunnaki invaders from a planet called Nibiru.

Today this area is known as Iraq and the occupation of the country had as much to do with concealing history as it did with oil.

The very first building US forces secured during their March 2003 invasion was the Iraqi National Museum in Baghdad. The second was the Iraqi National Bank. The latter was handed over to the Rorhschilds. The former was "looted" by the Illuminati of the many Sumerian artifacts it contained.

These relics provided valuable tools for New Science researchers who had just begun delving into the Sumerian clay tablets and their seemingly outrageous claims that Annunaki space invaders landed here to genetically engineer human slaves to work in their gold mines.

During this same period, Dubai, one of the emirates comprising the United Arab Emirates (UAE), became a duty-free port and drug money laundry serving much the same role as Hong Kong had for the City of London during the Vietnam War. This time the poppies for the Crown heroin were being sown in Afghanistan.

Where Hong Kong had financed Crown opium for arms swaps in the Golden Triangle, Dubai serves the City of London's smack -for-weapons trade in the Golden Crescent, an area comprised of parts of Iran, Afghanistan and Pakistan. Golden Crescent opium production eclipsed Golden Triangle production just as the CIA was manufacturing the *mujahideen* in Pakistan. Sharjah, another UAE emirate, has a duty-free airport specializing in covert weapons shipments.

The Gulf States of Saudi Arabia, UAE, Qatar, Bahrain, Oman and Kuwait are run by single-family monarchs who have been Muslim Brotherhood Crown Agents since the 1916 Sykes-Picot Agreement put them in power. Forty-two percent of the world's oil is contained within their borders. A year later, the Balfour Declaration sent to Lord Walter Rothschild paved the way for the creation of Israel, which is a Cabalistic Crown Agent.

Gold is the currency of drug and weapons traffickers and Dubai is a favorite hub in the global bullion trade. The British Bank of the Middle East dominates the Dubai gold trade. It is 100% owned by the world's largest bank, Hong Kong Shanghai Bank, better known as HSBC. Crown Agent HSBC monopolizes the Hong Kong gold trade along with Kleinwort Benson, which has close relations with Rio Tinto, a Crown company founded on Matheson family opium proceeds.

Matheson's heirs are the Keswick and Swire families, which dominate the board of directors at HSBC, Jardine Matheson, P&O Nedloyd and Cathay Pacific Airlines. Kleinwort's Sharps Pixley subsidiary is one of five firms that until 2007, gathered daily at N. M. Rothschild & Sons in London to unilaterally "fix" the price of gold.

Another of these gold fixers is Mocatta Metals, which is majority-owned by Standard Chartered, the bank Cecil Rhodes founded and where Lord Inchcape sits on the board. Mocatta is a favorite conduit for Israeli Mossad financing. Midland Bank subsidiary Samuel Montagu is a third London gold "fixer". Midland was bought by HSBC in 1999 and is partially owned by the Kuwaiti al-Sabah clan. The other two gold fixers are Johnson Matthey and N. M. Rothschild, both of which have interlocking boards with Anglo-American and HSBC.

Anglo-American is controlled by South Africa's Oppenheimer family who also own Engelhardt, which enjoys a monopoly in refining the world's gold. It was the mysterious Count of Saint-Germain who first claimed to possess the esoteric knowledge necessary for the transmutation of metals like gold and for removing flaws from diamonds.

The Count stayed for a time with William IX of Hesse, whose financial adviser was Mayer Rothschild. The Count may have imparted his secret wisdom upon young Mayer and his House of Hesse employer, who in partnership came to control the Cabalistic Frankfurt Freemason Lodge.

Diamonds are important in the laundering of drug money since they are small and easy to transport, yet hold great value. Sir Harry Oppenheimer's De Beers controls 85% of the global wholesale diamond market. De Beers is a subsidiary of Anglo-American where Sir Harry sits on the board. The current De Beers chairman is Nicky Oppenheimer.

De Beers' most valuable diamond mines are in southern Africa. One called Jwaneng, at the edge of the Kalahari Desert in Botswana, may be the most valuable property on earth. This vein of kimberlite produces diamonds and was only discovered in 1973.

De Beers also mines diamonds from platforms off the coast of Namibia. The world's largest store of diamonds sits under De Beers London headquarters. The company sells rough diamonds ten times a year in London to 125 hand-picked customers at a take-it-or-leave-it set price. De Beers was indicted in 1994 for price-fixing by the US Justice Department and to this day company officials do not set foot on US soil for fear they may be nabbed by US authorities.

Diamond cutting was, until recently, done in only two places in the world - Antwerp, Belgium and Ashqelon, Israel. In Antwerp the cutting was financed by Banque Bruxelles-Lambert, which is controlled by the Lambert family, cousins to the Rothschilds and owners of the scandal-ridden Drexel Burnham Lambert. In Israel, the cutting was financed by Bank Leumi – the biggest finance house in the country - and is controlled by the British Barclays Bank. Sir Harry Oppenheimer also sits on the Barclay's board. Recently, Gujarat, India, has become the location of choice for 90% of global diamond cutting due to the cheap labor it affords. Bangkok, Tel Aviv and New York handle the rest. Eighty-percent of diamond trading still occurs in Antwerp.

De Beers, like gold-fixer Standard Chartered, was founded by Cecil Rhodes in South Africa during the 1880's. Rhodes' last will and testament created the Royal Institute for International Affairs, which spawned the Council on Foreign Relations as its US Crown Agent. The main intent of the will is, "to establish a trust, to and for the establishment and promotion and development of a secret society, the true aim and object whereof shall be the extension of British rule throughout the world...and the ultimate recovery of the United States of America as an integral part of the British Empire."

Rhodes Scholars like Bill Clinton are funded by the Rhodes Trust. The principal trustee for the Rhodes estate is Lord Alfred Milner, who in 1899 provoked the Boer War through which Britain and Rhodes gained control over South Africa's diamond and gold mines. There, black South Africans toil in one of the world's most dangerous jobs and receive almost nothing for enriching the Oppenheimers and their cronies.

The world's three biggest mining companies: BHP Billiton, Rio Tinto and Anglo American are all controlled by the Crown Agent Oppenheimer/Rothschild/RD/Shell mob. In 2010 the first two talked of merging.

Canada is controlled by the Crown through the Bronfman family and their surrogates. Five huge Canadian banks and four large British banks that dominate the Caribbean Silver Triangle, a drug smugglers haven in which Belize and the Cayman Islands play key roles. The other Canadian banks are the Bank of Montreal, Royal Bank of Canada, Toronto Dominion Bank and Canadian Imperial Bank of Commerce. The British banks are National Westminster, Barclays, Lloyds and Midland Bank.

Midland was bought by HSBC and owns 20% of Standard Chartered Bank. These latter two banks print Hong Kong's money. Midland's board is loaded with ex-Pentagon officials who specialize in recycling petrodollars into CIA covert operations.

The Bank of Nova Scotia is the leading gold dealer in the Caribbean and the leading handler of capital flight out of the Caribbean. It is the banker of Noranda, a huge Canadian mining company that is the second largest dealer of gold in the Caribbean. Gold is the preferred currency of drug traffickers and Bank of Nova Scotia Jamaican subsidiary Scotiabank plays a huge role in the Caribbean drug trade. The 200 tons of gold recovered from vaults beneath the World Trade Center in the cleanup effort following the 911 terror attacks belonged to Bank of Nova Scotia.

Royal Bank of Canada has more off-shore subsidiaries than any other bank in the world. It bailed out the government of Guyana in 1976 after a CIA coup brought down the socialist government of Cheddi Jagan. Royal launched the business career of Venezuela's most powerful Cisneros family, which overseas Rockefeller interests in that country. Royal has a joint venture in the Bahamas with National Westminster called RoyWest.

Both the Bank of Nova Scotia and Royal Bank of Canada are controlled by Canada's most influential family - the Bronfmans. The Bronfmans control DuPont, which recently spun off Conoco, as well as Seagrams, Vivendi and Eagle Star Insurance.

Eagle Star is the Bronfman holding company and is a joint venture with British powerhouses Barclays, Lloyds, Hill Samuel and N. M. Rothschild & Sons. Eagle Star combined with Allianz Versicherung, a German company controlled by the von Thurn and Taxis and Wittelsbach families, to become a global titan in the area of finance.

The von Thurn and Taxis, Germany's deposed royal family, funded Tradition, Family and Property, the fascist movement responsible for right-wing death squad genocide throughout South America.

Eagle Star is close to British intelligence. Two current directors, Sir Kenneth Strong and Sir Kenneth Keith were #1 and #2 at British Intelligence during WWII. Keith is a director at Bank of Nova Scotia and chairman of Hill Samuel, where HSBC's Sir Philip de Zulueta joins Keith on the board. Keith is an influential member of the Canadian Institute for International Affairs (CIIA), the sister organization of London's powerful Royal Institute of International Affairs and the US Council on Foreign Relations. The official leader of Canada, by virtue of its Crown affiliation, is Britain's Queen Elizabeth II, whose mandates are carried out by a governor-general.

The Bank of Montreal has interlocking directorates with Seagrams and Hudson Bay Company. Hudson Bay is tight with Lord Inchcape's Peninsular & Orient Navigation Company (PONC) and the Hong Kong Keswick family that controls Jardine Matheson. PONC's Sir Eric Drake sits on the board at Hudson Bay. He and William Johnston Keswick also sit on the board of BP Amoco. Drake sits on the board of Kleinwort Benson, whose Sharps Pixley subsidiary runs 49% of the Hong Kong gold market. Keswick's son Henry Neville Lindley Keswick is a director at HSBC, Jardine Matheson and the Canadian paper giant MacMillan Bloedel, which merged with the largest US paper and timber company Weyerhaeuser in 1999.

MacMillan Bloedel took off when British Prime Minister Harold MacMillan married the daughter of Canada's Governor General Victor C. W. Cavendish, the 9th Duke of Devonshire. Canadian Pacific owns a controlling interest in MacMillan Bloedel.

Vancouver is a favorite drop point for SE Asian heroin on the way to the US. In 1978 Canadian intelligence officials were forced to admit in a Vancouver courtroom that Canadian Pacific Air flies most of Vancouver's heroin into the US. Canadian Pacific Railways is also involved.

All of these Canadian Silver Triangle interests have members of Queen Elizabeth II's secret modern-day roundtable, the Knights of St. John of Jerusalem, on their boards. At Canadian Pacific, board members J.C. Gilmar, J.P.W. Ostiguy, Charles Bronfman and W.E. McLaughlin are all Knights of St. John. McLaughlin also chairs Royal Bank of Canada.

Barclays has five Knights of St. John on its board, while Bank of Nova Scotia and Canadian Imperial Bank of Commerce have three Knights of Malta members each on their respective boards. Another Knight of Malta is Canadian Pacific board member M. G. Sandberg, who once chaired HSBC. Each of the big five Canadian banks have at least one Knight of Malta on their boards.

The CIIA is loaded with Knights of St. John as well. The CIIA's Honorary Chairman for life is Walter Lockhardt Gordon, whose father founded Clarkson & Gordon, the accounting firm that audits Toronto Dominion Bank, Bank of Nova Scotia and Canadian Imperial Bank of Commerce. CIIA board member Henry R. Jackman is a board member of the Italian Knights of St. John and the Order of Lazarus. Roland Michener, a former Canadian Governor General who chairs the CIIA, is a Knight of Malta.

During the Crusades, the Knights of St. John, also known as the Hospitallers, escorted European pilgrims into Jerusalem where King Solomon had built his Temple on Mount Moriah. The site is said to have housed the Ark of the Covenant and other sacred objects and secret documents. What remains of Solomon's Temple is housed today within the Al Aqsa Mosque on the Dome of the Rock, where the latest intifada began and always at the epicenter of Israeli/Palestinian tensions.

When the Dead Sea scrolls were discovered in 1947 at Qumran, one document etched in copper mentioned a huge treasure of gold buried beneath Solomon's Temple. This booty may explain why the Knights of St. John's brother organization, the Knights Templar, had turned over their pilgrim protection racket to the former group and focused their Crusade-era activity on excavating beneath the Temple. It would also explain how the Templars suddenly became the richest organization in the world.

Following their defeat by Muslim Saracens during the Crusades, the Knights of St. John fell back to the Mediterranean island of Cyprus, but in 1522 the Turks invaded and the twice-defeated

Knights relocated to Malta where the Roman Catholic faction became known as the Knights of Malta, today recognized as a sovereign nation by more than 40 countries. They are headquartered in Rome and answer to the Pope.

The protestant faction based in Britain is the Knights of St. John Jerusalem who answer to the Grand Prior of the Order, the Duke of Gloucester, cousin of Queen Elizabeth II.

Cecil Rhodes was a leader in European Freemasonry, where he mingled with the likes of the Rothschilds, King George IV, King William IV, Lord Randolph Churchill (Winston's father), the Marquis of Salisbury, Arthur Conan Doyle, Rudyard Kipling and Oscar Wilde. The group was preoccupied with the notion of an Aryan super-race, one they passed on to Adolf Hitler and the South African apartheid regime.

Their "secret knowledge" of human creation, which defies both creationist and evolutionist theories, is bound up in the tale of the Anunnaki who, according to recently uncovered Sumerian clay tablets, arrived around 6000 BC in Sumeria from planet Nibiru.

A growing number of researchers led by Zechariah Sitchin say the Anunnaki bred human slaves known in the Hebrew bible as Adamu and in English as Earthlings to mine gold necessary to patch up a hole in Nibiru's ozone layer caused by a collision with another planet.

One Anunnaki leader was named Nazi. According to the tablets, the alien gods who created Adam called their Mesopotamian colony E.DIN. They traveled the world in search of gold, which NASA scientists agree would be the best patch for our own ozone problem. Scientists have discovered mining operations going back as far as 100,000 BC in Africa, and South and Central America.

The Adamus who left Eden became gold mining slaves and their worldwide deployment may explain the many holes in evolutionary and anthropological theories of the day. It may also explain phenomena such as the Nazca Lines in Peru and the Great Pyramids of Egypt. Adam and his descendants became slaves to these Lords. The biblical Hebrew word *avodah*, commonly translated as "worship", actually means "to work". Adam and the biblical characters were not worshiping God, they were working for him as slaves. And "God" was the Anunnaki invaders.

The Sumerian tablets provide an intriguing explanation as to why man settled into agriculture in Mesopotamia from the much easier and more sustainable practice of hunting and gathering. The tablets state simply that the Anunnaki gods made them do it. Cities grew and the Anunnaki placed one of its god/human hybrids in charge of each new urban center. These rulers became Kings, their dynastic right to rule based on bloodlines to the Anunnaki.

The first such king was Cush, who was Noah's grandson and the father of Nimrod. Some researchers believe Yahweh himself was actually Anunnaki earth mission commander Enli, who was a brutal tyrant. Abraham, who all major religions claim as their patriarch, may have also been an Anunnaki hybrid.

The secret knowledge Abraham purveyed serves as the basis for all modern secret societies, from Freemasonry to Cabala to the Muslim Brotherhood. Whether true or not, what is important is that the Illuminati elite believe that these special bloodlines give them the God-given right to enslave all Earthlings.

By the mid-1890s, Freemason Cecil Rhodes launched the Diamond Syndicate whose successor, Central Selling Organization, still monopolizes the global diamond trade. Rhodes' forays were financed by the Rothschild family. In November 1997, Baron Edmond Rothschild died in Geneva and left in his trust substantial holdings in De Beers. According to former British Intelligence officer John Coleman, author of The Committee of 300, "Rhodes was principal agent for the Rothschilds [who] dispossessed the South African Boers of their birthright, the gold and diamonds that lay beneath their soil."

In 1888, Cecil Rhodes wrote his third will and left everything to Lord Rothschild. Rhodes, Milner and Rothschild founded the Business Roundtable in London in early 1900, which charted a course for expansion of the British Empire and for Crown control over the global economy.

CHAPTER 5

THE BUSINESS ROUNDTABLE

The Rothschilds exert political control through the secretive Business Roundtable, which they created in 1909 with the help of Lord Alfred Milner and South African industrialist Cecil Rhodes. The Rhodes Scholarship is granted by Cambridge University, out of which oil industry propagandist Cambridge Energy Research Associates operates. Cambridge Analytica also has its base here.

Rhodes founded De Beers and Standard Chartered Bank. Milner financed the Russian Bolsheviks on Rothschild's behalf, with help from Jacob Schiff and Max Warburg. In 1917 British Foreign Secretary Arthur Balfour penned a letter to Zionist Second Lord Lionel Walter Rothschild in which he expressed support for a Jewish homeland on Palestinian-controlled lands in the Middle East.

The Balfour Declaration justified the brutal seizure of Palestinian lands for the post-WWII establishment of Israel. Israel would serve, not as some high-minded "Jewish homeland", but as lynch pin in Rothschild/Eight Families control over the world's oil supply. Baron Edmond de Rothschild built the first oil pipeline from the Red Sea to the Mediterranean to bring BP Iranian oil to Israel. He founded

Israeli General Bank and Paz Oil. He is considered by many the father of modern Israel.

Roundtable inner Circle of Initiates included Lord Milner, Cecil Rhodes, Arthur Balfour, Albert Grey and Lord Nathan Rothschild. The Roundtable takes its name from the legendary knight of King Arthur, whose tale of the Holy Grail is paramount to the Illuminati notion of Sangreal or holy blood. According to former British Intelligence officer John Coleman, who wrote Committee of 300, "Round Tablers armed with immense wealth from gold, diamond and drug monopolies fanned out throughout the world to take control of fiscal and monetary policies and political leadership in all countries where they operated."

While Cecil Rhodes and the Oppenheimers went to South Africa, the Kuhn Loebs were off to re-colonize America. Rudyard Kipling was sent to India, the Schiffs and Warburgs manhandled Russia, while the Rothschilds, Lazards and Israel Moses Seifs pushed into the Middle East.

At Princeton, the Round Table founded the Institute for Advanced Study (IAS) as partner to its All Souls College at Oxford. IAS was funded by the Rockefeller's General Education Board. IAS members Robert Oppenheimer, Neils Bohr and Albert Einstein created the atomic bomb.

In 1919 Rothschild's Business Roundtable spawned the Royal Institute of International Affairs (RIIA) in London. The RIIA soon sponsored sister organizations around the globe, including the US Council on Foreign Relations (CFR), the Asian Institute of Pacific Relations, the Canadian Institute of International Affairs, the Brussels-based Institute des Relations Internationales, the Danish Foreign Policy Society, the Indian Council of World Affairs and the Australian Institute of International Affairs. Other affiliates popped up in France, Turkey, Italy, Yugoslavia and Greece.

The RIIA is a registered charity of the Queen and, according to its annual reports, is funded largely by the Four Horsemen of Oil - Exxon Mobil, Royal Dutch/Shell, Chevron Texaco and BP Amoco. Former British Foreign Secretary and Kissinger Associates co-founder Lord Carrington is President of both the RIIA and the

Bilderbergers. The inner circle at RIIA is dominated by Knights of St. John Jerusalem, Knights of Malta, Knights Templar and 33rd Degree Scottish Rite Freemasons.

The Knights of St. John were founded in 1070 and answer directly to the British House of Windsor. Their leading bloodline is the Villiers dynasty, which the Hong Kong Matheson family married into. The Lytton family also married into the Villiers gang. Colonel Edward Bulwer-Lytton led the English Rosicrucian secret society that Shakespeare opaquely referred to as Rosencranz, while the Freemasons took the role of Guildenstern. Lytton was spiritual father of both the RIIA and Nazi fascism. In 1871, he penned a novel titled, Vril: The Power of the Coming Race.

Seventy years later the Vril Society received ample mention in Adolf Hitler's Mein Kampf. Lytton's son became Viceroy to India in 1876 just before opium production spiked in that country. Lytton's good friend Rudyard Kipling introduced the the poppy to India and later worked under Lord Beaverbrook as Propaganda Minister, alongside Sir Charles Hambro of the Hambros banking dynasty.

James Bruce, ancestor to Scottish Rite Freemason founder Sir Robert the Bruce, was the 8th Earl of Elgin. He supervised the Caribbean slave trade as Jamaican Governor General from 1842-1846. He was Britain's Ambassador to China during the Second Opium War. His brother Frederick was Colonial Secretary of Hong Kong during both Opium Wars. Both were prominent Freemasons. British Lord Palmerston, who ran the Opium Wars, was a blood relative of the Bruce monarchy, as was his Foreign Secretary John Russell, grandfather of Bertrand Russell.

Children of the Roundtable elite are members of a Dionysian cult known as Children of the Sun. Initiates include Aldous Huxley, T. S. Eliot, D. H. Lawrence and H. G. Wells. Wells headed British intelligence during WWI. His books speak of a "one-world brain" and "a police of the mind". William Butler Yeats, another Sun member, was a pal of Aleister Crowley. The two formed an Isis Cult based on a Madam Blavatsky manuscript, which called on the British aristocracy to organize itself into an Isis Aryan priesthood.

Most prominent writers of English literature came from the ranks of the Roundtable. All promoted Empire expansion, however subtly. Blavatsky's Theosophical Society and Bulwer-Lytton's Rosicrucians joined forces to form the Thule Society out of which the Nazis emerged. Aleister Crowley formed the British parallel to the Thule Society, the Isis-Urania Hermetic Order of the Golden Dawn.

He tutored LSD guru Aldus Huxley who arrived in the US in 1952, the same year the CIA launched its MK-ULTRA mind control program with a little help from Warburg-owned Swiss Sandoz Laboratories and Rockefeller cousin Allen Dulles - OSS Station Chief in Berne. Dulles had also received information from the Muslim Brotherhood Saudi monarchy regarding the creation of mind-controlled Assassins. Dulles' assistant was James Warburg.

The Atlantic Union (AU) was an RIIA affiliate founded by Cecil Rhodes - who dreamed of returning the US to the British Crown. In 1939 AU set up its first offices in America in space donated by Nelson Rockefeller at 10 E 40th St in New York City. Every year from 1949-1976 an AU resolution was floored in Congress calling for a repeal of the Declaration of Independence and a "new world order". Today the group is on the forefront of pushing for war with Russia and Syria and calls itself the Atlantic Council.

Another RIIA affiliate was United World Federalists (UWF), founded by Norman Cousins and Dulles assistant James P. Warburg. UWF's motto was "One world or none". Its first president Cord Meyer stepped down to take a key position in Allen Dulles' CIA. Meyer articulated UWF's goal, "Once having joined the One-World Federated Government, no nation could secede or revolt...with the atom bomb in its possession the Federal Government would blow that nation off the face of the earth."

In 1950 UWF founder and Dulles' assistant James Warburg, whose elders Max and Paul sat on the board of Nazi business combine IG Farben, testified before the Senate Foreign Relations Committee, "We shall have world government whether or not you like it - by conquest or consent." The AU and UAF are close to the CFR and the Trilateral Commission (TC), founded by David Rockefeller and Zbigniew Brzezinski in 1974.

The TC published The Triangle Papers, which extended the "special relationship between the US and Western Europe" to include Japan, which was fast becoming creditor to the rest of the world. Former Federal Reserve Chairman Paul Volcker was TC Chairman. TC/CFR insider Harvard Professor Samuel Huntington, who most recently has argued for a "Clash of Civilizations" between the West and the Muslim world, wrote in the TC publication Crisis in Democracy, "...a government which lacks authority will have little ability short of cataclysmic crisis to impose on its people the sacrifices which may be necessary."

CHAPTER 6

THE CITY OF LONDON

Also known as the Crown, the one square mile City of London is contained within London proper and is a separate entity from both London and the UK. It has its own mayor, committeemen and aldermen. To be an alderman, one has to be a "Freeman" - code for Freemason. The world's biggest Freemason lodge is contained within the City. Thus, all the perverted regalia its managers wear.

Every prominent bank in the world has a branch in the City and it is here where all derivatives in the world trade from. The City was founded in the 11th Century under the Magna Carta agreement made by the European nobility.

When Knights Templar Jacques de Molay was burned alive by Pope Clemente for being a Satanist, the Holy Roman Empire loaded up its ill-gotten wealth and moved their headquarters to the City of London.

Thus the Roman Empire never died. It just relocated. Nor did the British Empire die. They both operate now from the City of London.

The Anglican Church is here and its bishops are instrumental in giving religious cover to the Satanists who rule the City. The entire offshore banking network of the world is run from here, since there is no regulation or transparency. The Bank of England sits within the City, shielding the identity of the owners of these dirty money tax-free accounts in places like the Cayman Islands, Panama, Curacao, the Isle of Man and the Isle of Jersey.

"Freeport" status is granted from here, making all ships registered in either Liberia or Panama exempt from taxation from either the country of origin or the country of destiny for all goods. Freeport, Bahamas holds a similar status.

The voters in the City include the banks themselves. There is no democracy here and even Queen Elizabeth II must bow before the City mayor before entering, then walk behind him while inside its confines.

The Crown used its Bridge Fund to socially engineer entire nations via the Tavistock Institute. It's media arm is the BBC, run out of Chatham House. Its foreign policy/war making arm is the Royal Institute for International Affairs (RIIA). It's historical lie department is the Royal Geographical Society. And its vampire branch is the Red Cross (Red Shield of Rothschild), which gets people to donate blood, then sells it for hundreds of dollars a pint to people in need of it.

The Crown's financial repository is headquartered at the Bank of International Settlements (BIS) in Basel, Switzerland. There is a reason why Switzerland is not part of the EU. There is also a reason the Crown is behind the Brexit. The Satanists like to herd others into unions of all sorts, but they always remain free of any possible democratic interference in the hegemony.

Interestingly, Basel lies half way between Rome and London. This is very convenient for the Holy Roman empire bankers who moved their loot to London when deMolay was burned by Pope Clemente on Friday the 13th since most of the old Genoese banking families still lived in northern Italy.

This also explains why the British are constantly portrayed as smarter than the rest of us, often narrating documentaries and broadcasting news. The City wants Americans to be Anglophiles so that we won't suspect the fleecing that is being done to us.

For the same reason, Italy is portrayed in the Tavistock media as a treasure trove of knowledge and culture - a must visit country for every American. Personally, it was one of my least favorite countries of the 50 I have traveled to. But Americans are constantly being pushed to visit this cradle of Satanism. Tuscany is Tavistock's latest tourist "program".

Egyptology as a study is promoted for the same reason, because it was the Grand Lodge of Cairo that spawned this Luciferian Brotherhood of the Snake, which moved first to Rome then to London. The bankers write history.

BIS oversees and controls the planet's private central banks, including the US Federal Reserve. It is said that around 8,000 Illuminati run the BIS, though I think the number may be much smaller. For more on this see my book *The Federal Reserve Cartel*.

Every nation's central bank falls under BIS control, except Cuba, Iran, Syria, Sudan and North Korea. Libya's did not until Qaddafi was murdered and replaced with City stooges.

"Free Trade" is the mantra of these Satanists, and those working for the City of London are known as Crown Agents. The East India Company was an earlier version of this. Nowadays, the Crown has its agents in every country in the world.

In the US Henry Kissinger has played a key Crown Agent role in the foreign policy arena. In recent times George Soros has been the most prominent Crown Agent, engineering currency collapses, fake colored revolutions, the Arab Spring and wars worldwide. Soros also plays this role domestically in the US in the social engineering sphere. His cover is known as the Open Society Foundation. Foundations are the way the oligarchs launder money, while steering social, economic and foreign policy.

Kissinger Associates clients included the Bank of Credit & Commerce International, BCCI-owned National Bank of Georgia, and Banca Nacional de Lavoro (BNL), which worked with the Iraqi Central Bank to arm Iraq through numbered accounts at Bank of America, Bank of New York, Chase Manhattan and Manufacturers Hanover Trust. BNL's clearing agent on these transactions was Morgan Guaranty Trust. The Rockefeller-controlled JP Morgan

Chase Board of Directors mirrors BNL's Consulting Board for International Policy.

Henry Kissinger is tight with both Chase Manhattan and Goldman Sachs, which helped the drug-infested Bank of New York and CS First Boston loot Russia's Treasury in 1998. When the CIA mob was done looting the S&Ls in 1988, Goldman Sachs swooped up billions in assets for a song. JP Morgan Chase's International Advisory Board includes Y. K. Pao of Hong Kong Worldwide Shipping, Ian Sinclair of the Canadian Pacific heroin express and G. A. Wagner of Royal Dutch/Shell. Pao is Vice-Chairman at HSBC - the world's biggest and dirtiest bank based in the City.

Kissinger Associates' board is even more shadowy and powerful, a Masonic Freudian slip since "Kiss Ass" is what the brethren do when old money talks. Co-founder Lord Carrington, board member at both Barclays and Hambros, chairs both the Bilderberger Group and the Royal Institute for International Affairs. Kiss Ass board member Mario d'Urso of the Kuhn Loeb banking dynasty heads Jefferson Insurance - the US joint venture of Assicurazioni Generali (AG) and Riunione Adriatica di Sicurta (RAS).

AG of Venice is keeper of the immense fortunes of the old Venetian banking families who funded the Crusades and the Holy Roman Empire. Its board included Elie de Rothschild; Baron August Von Finck, the richest man in Germany; Baron Pierre Lambert, Rothschild, cousin and the money behind Drexel Burnham Lambert; Jocelyn Hambro, whose family owns Hambros Bank, which owned half of Michelle Sindona's Banca Privata; Pierpaolo Luzzatto Fequiz of the powerful Italian Luzzato family, which had ties to Michelle Sindona's Banco Amrosiano; and Frano Orsini Bonacossi of the powerful Orsini family, whose members sat in the original Roman Empire Senate. The biggest shareholders of AG are Lazard Freres and Banque Paribas.

Paribas is controlled by the Warburg family, while Lazard is dominated by the Lazard and David-Weill families. The British Lazards are now part of the Pearson conglomerate that owns *The Financial Times*, *The Economist*, Penguin and Viking Books, Madame Tussaud's, and has extensive US interests. The French Lazard Freres is tucked under a holding company known as EuraFrance. Lazard handles money for the global elite including the Italian Agnellis, the Belgian Boels, the British Pearsons and the American Kennedys.

RAS board members include members of the Giustiniani family, who descend from Roman Emperor Justinian; members of the Dora family, Genoese financiers of the Spanish Hapsburg monarchs; and the Duke of Alba, who descends from the Spanish Hapsburg monarchy.

Another powerhouse on the Kiss Ass board was Nathaniel Samuels, an old Kuhn Loeb hand from the Samuel clan that controls much of Royal Dutch/Shell and Rio Tinto. Samuels was Chairman of the Paris-based Banque Louis-Dreyfus Holding Company, which descends from the Louis Dreyfus grain trading dynasty - one of the Four Horsemen of Grain (Cargill, Bunge, Andre and Louis Dreyfus). Lord Eric Roll is another board member at KissAss. Roll is chairman of the Warburg family investment bank S. G. Warburg.

The Kiss Ass Asian powerhouse board member is Sir Y. K. Kan of Hong Kong, who represents four old money Chinese families that control the Bank of East Asia. Kiss Ass client BNL's P-2 Freemason roots can be traced back to Banca Commerciale d'Italia, where P-2 was founded. The bank's Swiss subsidiary Banca de la Svizzera bought 7% of Lehman Brothers in the mid-1970's. The Lehman family made their fortune running guns to Confederate forces while smuggling southern British opium family plantation cotton to the Union. When Lehman Brothers client Enron collapsed, UBS Warburg swooped in to seize Enron OnLine for $0.

The Crown Killed Kennedy

Clint Murchison had meat packing interests in Haiti that were looked after by CIA agent George de Mohrenschildt, a wealthy Russian oilman and, according to the FBI, a Nazi spy during WWII. It was de Mohrenschildt who drove Lee Harvey Oswald from New Orleans to Dallas days before the November 22, 1963 assassination of President John F. Kennedy. Gaeton Fonzi, a special investigator for the House Select Committee on Assassinations, was on his way to interview de Mohrenschildt in Florida regarding his role in the JFK hit when the CIA agent was found with a shotgun blast through his head. De Mohrenschildt's diaries were later uncovered. One entry read, "Bush, George H. W. (Poppy), 1412 W Ohio also Zapata Petroleum Midland".

Kennedy had done plenty to piss off the US military establishment. In October 1963 he pulled 1,000 advisers out of SE Asia and issued NSAM 363, a blueprint for a total Vietnam withdrawal. He sent US Ambassador to Guinea William Atwood to Cuba to begin talks with Fidel Castro after publicly blasting the CIA's bungling of the Bay of Pigs operation.

Kennedy said he wanted to "splinter the CIA into a thousand pieces and scatter it to the winds" and that he understood Castro's revolutionary struggle against dictator and Meyer Lansky crony Fulgencio Batista, who Kennedy called, "an incarnation of a number of sins on the part of the US".

Ted Shackley, Santos Trafficante and the CIA boys running Operation Mongoose, which aimed to assassinate Castro, were especially outraged at Kennedy. Major General Edward Lansdale had commandeered Operation Mongoose and escalated it into a small war against Cuba.

In 1955 Lansdale helped Lucien Conein set up the South Vietnamese Opium Monopoly under President Nguyen Cao Ky. The CIA continued to train anti-Castro rebels in south Florida and around Lake Ponchartrain outside New Orleans, even after JFK had the FBI raid these CIA camps.

Kennedy fired CIA Director and Rockefeller cousin Allen Dulles, CIA Deputy Director Charles Cabell (whose brother was the mayor of Dallas) and CIA Deputy Director of Plans Richard Bissell. Richard Helms was Bissell's successor at the Company's dirty tricks bureau, as the Plans section was known.

Helms was tight with James "Jesus" Angleton, who ran the CIA's MK-ULTRA mind control program for years, possibly utilizing information Dulles had obtained in Switzerland from the House of Saud Muslim Brotherhood.

All the Watergate plumbers came from an Operation Mongoose offshoot known as Operation 40. Plumber Howard Hunt was paymaster for Operation 40, which also included plumbers Bernard Barker and Enterprise liaison Rafael Quintero. Plumber Frank Sturgis ran the Miami-based International Anti-Communist Brigade, which was funded by Santos Trafficante through his Teamsters Local 320 front. The other Watergate burglars were Felipe Diego and Rolando Martinez. They were buddies with OSS China hand William Pawley, who had owned sugar refineries in Cuba as well as the country's bus line.

Hunt ran the Miami based Double-Chek, a CIA channel during the Bay of Pigs. Sturgis physically attacked Vietnam War opponent Daniel Ellsberg on the steps of the Capitol and recruited agent provocateurs to disrupt peaceful protests at the 1972 Democratic Convention. As part of Operation 40 Frank Sturgis recruited Marita Lorenz to seduce Castro, then kill him.

Miss Lorenz says she rode to Dallas in a vehicle loaded with weapons with Frank Sturgis, Jerry Patrick Hemming, two Cuban exile brothers named Novis and a pilot named Pedro Diaz Lanz. Lorenz says they arrived in Dallas the day before Kennedy was shot, where they met Howard Hunt at a local hotel.

Fletcher Prouty was an Air Force intelligence officer who had been part of Kennedy's fact-finding mission that resulted in the NSAM 263 directive calling for a US pullout of Vietnam. On November 10, 1963 Prouty's boss Edward Lansdale reassigned him to a South Pole desk job. Twelve days later Kennedy was assassinated.

Prouty swears that a photograph of Dealey Plaza on the day of the assassination shows Edward Lansdale walking away from the scene of the crime. Others have identified Howard Hunt as one of the tramps who lurked on the railroad tracks behind the grassy knoll from where the fatal shot was fired.

George Bush Sr. headed Houston-based Zapata Offshore Petroleum from 1956-1964. According to authors William Cooper and David Icke, in 1961 Zapata got the CIA into the Colombian cocaine business.

Zapata's offshore oil platforms were used to transship cocaine, while the Four Horsemen of Oil (Exxon Mobil, Royal Dutch/Shell, BP Amoco and Chevron Texaco) shipped chemicals to Columbia necessary in the production of coke. One CIA operation to invade Cuba was code-named Operation Zapata. The two Navy ships used in the attempt were named Barbara and Houston.

An FBI memo from J. Edgar Hoover dated 11-23-63 discusses briefing "George Bush of CIA" on the Kennedy assassination, which had occurred one day earlier. Bush was in Dallas on November 22nd. One intelligence source stated, "I know he (Bush) was involved in the Caribbean. I know he was involved in the suppression of things after the Kennedy assassination".

In a 1973 interview published in the Atlantic Monthly, Kennedy Vice-President and successor Lyndon Johnson, himself a Texas oilman, hinted at a conspiracy on that gloomy day in Dallas and talked of a "Murder Incorporated" being run by the CIA out of the Caribbean. Johnson was referring to Permindex (Permanent Industrial Exhibitions), an assassination bureau run by the Special Operations Executive (SOE) of Britain's MI6.

According to a book published by Executive Intelligence Review called Dope Inc., Permindex was funded by the Canadian Bronfman family and the wealthy Polish Solidarist Radziwill family. Permindex leader, MI6 SOE Colonel Sir William "Intrepid" Stephenson, had earlier deployed the Meyer Lansky syndicate and helped rehabilitate Lucky Luciano.

SOE Colonel Louis Mortimer Bloomfield was an OSS veteran and Bronfman liaison who chaired Permindex since its 1958 founding in Montreal and Geneva. SOE and Permindex insider General Julius Klein ran guns to the murderous Haganah when the Zionists seized Israel from the Palestinians. He now "handles" Buffalo mob boss Max Fischer and Carl Lindner at United Brands.

Other SOE members included David Sarnoff, whose RCA conglomerate at that time formed the core of the US National Security Agency; and Walter Sheridan, who provided intelligence to Resorts International and fugitive financier Robert Vesco.

RCA was later bought by General Electric, whose spin-off SERCO now serves as the Crown Agent that sponges exclusive contracts from the US State and Defense Departments, all branches of the US military and FEMA Region 9.

The most familiar member of Crown-controlled SOE was Colonel Clay Shaw, whose son of same name became a Florida Congressman serving on a House Narcotics Task force. Shaw was an OSS veteran who later became Director of the New Orleans International Trade Mart, the US subsidiary of Permindex. Shaw was indicted in 1969 for his role in the Kennedy assassination by New Orleans attorney Jim Garrison. During the trial seventeen key prosecution witnesses died and Garrison became the target of a smear campaign.

According to Dope Inc., Shaw served under Stephenson for twenty years starting in WWII, where he had been OSS liaison to Winston Churchill. SOE operatives infiltrated the FBI and formed Division Five, a British intelligence Fifth Column that was headed by Bloomfield. Both Bloomfield and Shaw were present at a series of meetings in Montego Bay, Jamaica in 1963. The meetings were held at the Tyndall Compound, built by Sir William Stephenson to serve British intelligence interests in the Caribbean after WWII.

Stephenson had launched BRINCO, an energy exploration firm financed by the Oppenheimer family's Rio Tinto. He moved to Jamaica in 1949 and set up the British-American-Canadian Corporation with financing from UK merchant banking giant Hambros. It was Stephenson who helped Allen Dulles stash the Hitler and Goebell trusts in Swiss bank accounts after WWII. Now he presided over the Montego Bay meetings where, according to many Kennedy assassination researchers, the JFK hit was planned.

Those present at the meetings included Ferenc Nagy, a WWII cabinet minister in the pro-Hitler Horthy government of Hungary, who later became Hungarian Prime Minister; Georgio Mantello, a Romanian emigre who served as Italian dictator Benito Mussolini's Trade Minister; Paul Raigoradsky, a Russian Solidarity leader; and Jean de Menil, an old money European aristocrat and Russian president of Schlumberger, the giant oil industry service provider and frequent CIA arms conduit based in Houma, LA.

All present at Tyndall were executives of Permindex, whose board members included Donald Trump's mentor Roy Cohn, former general counsel to Sen. Joe McCarthy; Montreal crime boss Joe Bonnano; Mussolini Agriculture Minister Count Guitierez de Spadafora of the Italian House of Savoy; Hapsburg and Wittelsbach family banker Hans Seligman of Basel; Carlo d'Amelio, Rome attorney for the Houses of Savoy and Pallavicini; King Farouk of Egypt's uncle Munir Chourbagi; and Guiseppe Zigiotti, head of the Italian Fascist Association for Militia Arms. Permindex was a front for the Crown's Nazi International.

Colonel Louis Bloomfield was a partner at Philips, Vineberg, Bloomfield and Goodman - attorneys for the Canadian Bronfman family. In 1968 the firm was forced to delete Bloomfield's name from its letterhead when French President Charles de Gaulle publicly exposed Bloomfield for his role in an assassination attempt on de Gaulle. de Gaulle named Credit Suisse of Geneva as financier of Bloomfield's attempted putsch and traced its origin to NATO Headquarters in Brussels.

Permindex was forced to move its offices out of Europe to fascist-friendly South Africa. Simultaneously, de Gaulle kicked the Israeli Mossad out of France due to its cozy relations with Permindex. Credit Suisse Canada has been identified by some researchers as SOE paymaster for the Permindex assassination of JFK, which was accomplished after Stephenson set up an operations command center in David Sarnoff's RCA Building at New York's Rockefeller Center.

Bloomfield worked under the cover of Israeli Continental Corporation and the Canadian subsidiary of Heineken Breweries. He controls the Ran Histadrut "charity", which constitutes 33% of Israel's GNP; and Bank Hapoalim, Israel's second largest bank and a favorite Mossad conduit. Bloomfield was director of the Israeli-Canadian Maritime League and served as Canadian Consul-General in the "free port" nation Liberia.

There he worked with the only other foreign diplomat in the Monrovia, Banque du Credit Internacionale's (BCI) Tibor Rosenbaum, in establishing Liberia's status as an off-shore banking center and in making Liberia's flag available to international shippers who wished to disguise their true country of origin. The Liberian flag has been well utilized by the Crown's drugs and arms smugglers.

Bloomfield was also chairman of the Red Cross Ambulance Service, a post traditionally held by the top Knight in Queen Elizabeth II's modern-day roundtable - Most Venerable Military & Hospitalier Order of St. John of Jerusalem. Though known for its more charitable side, which includes selling donated blood for around $700/pint, the Red Cross is officially an intelligence arm of the Crown.

According to Dope Inc., Tibor Rosenbaum's BCI was a key bank in the Permindex assassination of Kennedy, transferring funds from Bank Hapoalim to New Orleans FBI Division Five Station Chief Guy Bannister.

Bannister's agent Jerry Brooks Gaitlin doled out the cash to Hunt and his Cuban team of assassins. Both Bannister and Gaitlin died under mysterious circumstances. Howard Hunt's Double Chek was a subsidiary of Centro Mondiale Commerciale - the Permindex Rome branch. William Seymour, the Oswald double who played Cuban sympathizer for months before the Kennedy hit, met with Clay Shaw and David Ferrie to form the triangulation of fire plan. The actual Oswald was also on SOE Division Five payroll.

According to many researchers, the weapons for the Kennedy coup came through Schlumberger and the seven-shooter hit team consisted of an elite group put together by J. Edgar Hoover and Sir William Stephenson in 1943. The team was formed through the American Council of Christian Churches (ACCC), which Bloomfield, Stephenson and Hoover had founded as a cover for US and British intelligence via ACCC Latin American missions.

ACCC is a network of aristocratic far-right religions. Its west coast director E. E. Bradley was indicted by New Orleans prosecutor Jim Garrison for his role in the JFK hit. David Ferrie worked under

ACCC cover. An ACCC orphan school near Puebla, Mexico was used to train 25-30 of the world's premier marksmen.

ACCC Minister Albert Osborne ran the school after he fled the US due to his support of Hitler during WWII. These "students" carried out the Kennedy assassination. Assassins from this same team may have deployed to kill both Bobby Kennedy and Martin Luther King Jr.

Kennedy was scheduled to speak at the Dallas Trademart, a Permindex affiliate, the day he was gunned down. After the Kennedy assassination Permindex morphed into Intertel, while BCI was replaced by Robert Vesco's Bahamas-based Resorts International, whose lawyers included Paul Helliwell and Kennedy Justice Department hack Robert Peloquin, who served in Naval Intelligence and with NSA before joining Justice.

In 1987 Donald Trump bought 93% of Resorts International before being bailed out of bankruptcy in 1992 by Rothschild Inc. bond specialist Wilbur Ross - now Secretary of Commerce.

Resorts has its headquarters on Paradise Island, which is owned by Huntington Hartford, scion of the Great Atlantic and Pacific Tea Company. Intertel is officially a subsidiary of Resorts and its board included Howard Hunt buddy Edward Mullin of FBI Division Five, the president of the Bronfman family-controlled Royal Bank of Canada, David Belisle of NSA and Sir Randolph Bacon, former head of Scotland Yard. Intertel provides security for Caribbean and Las Vegas casinos and moved gambling and horse racing into Atlantic City, NJ after strawman Donald Trump bought up the boardwalk.

The Warren Commission that "investigated" the Kennedy assassination was stacked with the very cronies Kennedy had denounced. Allen Dulles, the CIA Director whom Kennedy had fired, loomed large over the proceedings, steering the inquiry away from any hint of CIA involvement. FBI Director J. Edgar Hoover was a right-wing fanatic who despised Kennedy. President Gerald Ford, then a Michigan Senator, leaked information on the hearings to FBI Assistant Director Cartha De Loach. Senators Arlen Spector (D-PA) and Richard Shelby (R-AL) were prominent members of the Senate Intelligence Committee, which oversees CIA activity.

But the most influential member of the Warren Commission was Chase Manhattan Bank chairman John McCloy, who later directed the World Bank. McCloy was attorney for the Saudi-based ARAMCO and helped David Rockefeller spirit the Shah out of Iran. Kennedy had angered the US military establishment but his death sentence was signed by the international bankers.

Kennedy had announced a crackdown on off-shore tax havens and proposed increases in tax rates on large oil and mining companies. He supported eliminating tax loopholes that benefit the super-rich. His economic policies were publicly attacked by *Fortune* magazine, the *Wall Street Journal* and both David and Nelson Rockefeller. Even Kennedy's own Treasury Secretary Douglas Dillon, who came from the Bechtel-controlled Dillon Read investment bank, voiced opposition to the JFK proposals.

Kennedy's fate was sealed in June 1963 when he authorized the issuance of more than $4 billion in United States Notes by his Treasury Department in an attempt to circumvent the high interest rate usury of the Crown's private Federal Reserve international banker crowd. President Lincoln had made a similar move 100 years earlier and suffered the same consequences.

The wife of accused assassin Lee Harvey Oswald, who was conveniently gunned down by Jack Ruby before Ruby himself was shot, told author A. J. Weberman in 1994, "The answer to the Kennedy assassination is with the Federal Reserve Bank. Don't underestimate that. It's wrong to blame it on Angleton and the CIA *per se* only. This is only one finger on the same hand. The people who supply the money are above the CIA".

New Orleans Trade Mart Director and SOE operative Clay Shaw's address book contained the names of many powerful people who may have "supplied the money". They included international oligarchs Maquesse Guiseppe Rey of Italy, Baron Rafaelo de Banfield of Italy, Princess Jaqueline Chimay of France, Lady Margaret D'Arcy of England, Lady Hulce of England and Sir Michael Duff of England.

But the most interesting phone number in Shaw's address book belonged to Sir Steven Runciman, an elite historian with insider knowledge of the Knights Templar and their Priory of Sion inner sanctum. Warren Commission Chairman Earl Warren, John McCloy, Allen Dulles, J. Edgar Hoover and Gerald Ford were all 33rd Degree Illuminized Freemasons.

Visitors to the Dealey Plaza assassination site report seeing an obelisk dedicated to Freemasonry. Dallas, headquarters for illumination merchant Exxon Mobil and much of corporate America, sits on the 33rd parallel.

The Crown Was Behind 911

The Crown had the most to gain from dialing 911. The day of the terror attacks there was an unusually heavy volume of financial transactions being handled at the WTC. The bulk of investment bankers killed in the WTC worked for competitors of the Big Six old money investment banks. Cantor Fitzgerald was particularly hard hit.

Merrill Lynch had its own building nearby, as did Deutsche Bank. Lehman Brothers moved from the WTC to a newly built headquarters just prior 911. Only seven weeks before 911 a group of wealthy oligarch investors terminated their lease on the WTC. Investor Larry Silverstein bought a 99-year lease on the property in July 2001, while the old money slid out from under it.

Silverstein filed a $7.2 billion insurance claim after the tragedy. The Federal Reserve-controlling Eight Families (Rothschild, Rockefeller, Kuhn Loeb, Lazard Freres, Warburg, Israel Moses Seif, Lehman/Oppenheimer and Goldman Sachs) insurance companies involved offered only $3.6 billion.

The President's brother Marvin was on the board of directors at Securacom - now known as Stratesec Inc. - from 1993-2000. The company provided security for the WTC, Dulles International Airport and United Airlines. It had the security contract at Los Alamos Laboratories, when there had been a number of security breaches at that facility.

The firm is backed by a Kuwaiti-American investment firm known as KuwAm. Current clients include the US Army, US Navy,

US Air Force and Department of Justice. They carry a Blanket Purchase Agreement with the GSA - meaning no other company can compete for these security contracts.

According to David Icke's bombshell book *Children of the Matrix*, Securacom is a subsidiary of Crown Agency - a British Crown entity that Icke says also owns the Agha Khan Foundation. Khan founded the modern Muslim Brotherhood and is spiritual torch-bearer for Islamism - from which groups like Al Qaeda and the Taliban take their cues. This important fact points to Buckingham Palace involvement in the prosecution of 911.

Marvin Bush also sat on the board at HCC Insurance Holdings until November 2002. That company carried some of the insurance on the WTC. Brother Jeb - Governor of Florida - declared a state of emergency in his state one week prior to 911. He personally escorted the alleged hijackers' flight school documents to Washington, DC shortly after the attacks.

New York Mayor Rudolf Guliani was portrayed as hero of 911. Yet on November 2, 2001 Guliani ordered New York firefighters to thin their ranks at ground zero, as the WTC carnage became known. The day before, 200 tons of gold buried in vaults beneath the WTC belonging to Silver Triangle gold kingpin Bank of Nova Scotia was recovered.

No one in the fawning corporate media bothered to ask Guliani about the callous timing of his decision. Nor did they ask him why, according to Internet reports, he had ordered 6,000 gallons of fuel stored in WTC #7 to supply his personal bomb shelter. The explosion of this fuel may have caused WTC #7 - which was clearly not hit by an airplane - to collapse, destroying sensitive Enron-related CIA and FBI documents stored there. The CIA ran an undercover station on the 47th floor of #7. The 23rd and 24th floors of the WTC North Tower housed FBI covert operations and boatloads of agency documents.

Louie Cacchioli, a firefighter with Engine 47 in Harlem said he was in an elevator to the spook-occupied 24th floor of the North Tower, when he heard explosions. His crew - the first in that building - believes bombs were set off inside the towers.

In a statement to *The Albuquerque Journal* shortly after the disaster, Van Romero - Vice-President for Research at the renowned New Mexico Institute for Mining and Technology - agreed. Romero, one of the world's foremost demolitions experts, stated, "My opinion is, based on the videotapes, that after the airplanes hit the World Trade Center there were some explosive devices inside the buildings that caused the towers to collapse."

Numerous experts also agreed that jet fuel alone burns too fast to have melted the massive steel structure of the WTC on its own. The orderly nature of the collapse of both towers and later pancake collapse of Building #7 cry out for inquiry.

The contractor awarded the $7 billion job of cleaning up the WTC rubble was eerily named Controlled Demolition - the same outfit that quickly disposed of the evidence of the Alfred T. Murrah Federal Building after the Oklahoma City bombing.

WTC "scrap metal" was expeditiously shipped to China. Brigham Young physics Professor Steven Jones, who studied the WTC rubble, says he found traces of thermite explosives all over the stuff. In September 2006, Brigham Young placed Jones on paid leave for his efforts at seeking truth.

In the weeks before 911 people working at the WTC reported entire floors being shut door for "elevator maintenance" It had to be Securacom that authorized this closing and it was during this time that the Crown Agents must have been busy mining the elevator shafts.

There is a persistent rumor that all Israelis working at the WTC were instructed not to report to work on 911. Was Time's 2001 Man of the Year and current Trump advisor Rudy Guliani part of a covert operation to consolidate British/Israeli/Rothschild control over Persian Gulf Oil? It was probably no coincidence that Guliani was Knighted by Queen Elizabeth II in February 2002.

It was is also convenient that Crown Agent SERCO has current contracts through the FAA to run numerous air traffic control at major airports. SERCO, owned by British Knights, also has contracts with every branch of the US military, the Defense Department and the State Department. It regularly receives no bid contracts by using

Crown Agents within the US government know as Senior Executive Services (SES). SERCO is a spin-off from the old RCA Kennedy assassins via that latter's takeover by General Electric. Both SERCO and GE have close ties to both Lockheed Martin and British Aerospace, the world's two biggest defense contractors. All are Crown Agents.

SERCO is the mechanism through which the City of London both creates war, then profits from the resulting contracts. In Britain they own a pathology company that some believe is poised to profit from the coming depopulation of 75% of the world's people, a major goal of the Crown Satanists. SERCO also holds a contract to run FEMA Region 9 in the US.

This region contains Arizona, Nevada, California, Hawaii and the Pacific Islands. As I write this, Kilauea Volcano is erupting. A company called Puna Geothermal Venture, which is financially connected to the Rothschilds, has been fracking near the Puna Geothermal Power Station. Why?

Puna Geothermal Ventures is owned by Ormat Industries, an Israeli firm found by Lucien Yehuda Bronicki. In 1977 Bronicki was awarded with the Rothschild Prize for Innovation/Export.

According to a 5-15-18 article on *Exopolitics.org* by Big Island resident Michael Salla, independent journalist Hal Turner says he had been contacted by scientists with the US Geological Survey. They told Turner that an area of land on the south flank of the volcano known as the Hilina Slump - about the size of Manhattan - is moving and could break off into the ocean, sending a Tsunami toward the west coast with 100+ foot waves moving at 500 miles per hour. Cities like San Diego, Los Angeles and could be wiped off the face of the earth.

God forbid, should this occur, that SERCO FEMA Region 9 contract will be worth billions to the Luciferian Crown.

CHAPTER 7

THE SOCIAL DARWINISM FRAUD

It is important to understand the historical transition of the methodology employed by the Illuminati in their never-ending quest to control the people and resources of planet earth.

Paramount is the shift from open confrontation with and violent suppression of liberation movements, to more subtle forms of psychological warfare-waged control and distortion of information through the mass media. Perception management is the name of the game.

This battle for our minds takes many forms, but begins by inserting key philosophical premises into the public consensus. One of the most insidious of these is social Darwinism, which preaches "survival of the fittest" and reinforces the top-down dominance paradigm. This fraudulent Luciferian world view - reinforced by corporate-funded "scientific" research - needs to be deconstructed and discredited if we are to progress as a species.

Charles Darwin's expedition was funded by European nobility. He was himself a Freemason. Despite this elite pedigree, Darwin's research led him to one very important conclusion, and it was not the "survival of the fittest" mantra that the global elite have since employed to justify everything from colonialism and slavery to private central banking and monopoly capitalism. Rather, Darwin's central thesis was that the survival of a species was dependent on a high degree of cooperation within that species.

I grew up on a 2,000 acre ranch and have lived in the country almost my entire life. I have hunted, trapped, fished, raised livestock and had pets. I have hiked countless miles of back country Montana trails where I've encountered grizzly bears, mountain goats, moose and wolverine. My wife and I recently went on a safari in South Africa's Kruger National Park.

Through all of these experiences I have never seen two wild animals locked in mortal combat. What I have seen is cooperation at many levels, not only within species, but between species. Yet if you watch any Royal Geographic Society-funded documentary on wildlife, the theme of conflict is omnipresent.

Take a walk in the woods and you will hear songbirds warning the fox that you are headed her way. Observe a herd of deer and you will see the fit, healthy individuals watching out and waiting for the young, injured or sick members. Visit Kruger and you will see warthogs sticking close to the zebras. The zebras can see above the bushveld and watch for lions, while the smaller warthogs, with their razor-sharp tusks, can give a lion problems for long enough to allow a zebra to escape an ambush.

I had two dogs for nearly fifteen years. Buck, the larger dog, deferred to Milo, the smaller but older dog, his entire life. They never once had a physical confrontation. Though Buck was easily the stronger of the two, he saw no need to be the "big dog". Buck knew that cooperation was a much easier path. In turn Milo never abused his respected position of "elder".

I later adopted a family of three male cats. When Bob caught a mouse, he would often give it to Loris. When Loris caught one he would give it to Harvey. We used to wait in anticipation to see if they would fight over it, but they never did. Often they would triangulate and hunt together, while also keeping a lookout for bigger predators.

Of course confrontation occurs in the animal community, mostly during the rut and when food is scarce. Boys will be boys. And all living beings must eat. But why does the Tavistock perception management media focus so much on these rare incidents and so little on the much more prevalent cooperation within the natural community? Because doing so would shatter the myth that monopoly capitalism is a natural economic system.

Greed is not natural. Cooperation is. We are inherently loving.

The global elite have utilized this same phony version of neo-Darwinism in their portrayal of indigenous people. We are told, usually when justifying some oil war for Exxon Mobil or Citibank, that "Indians were constantly at war (blah, blah, blah),too." Yet any cultural anthropologist worth their salt will tell you that Native Americans rarely waged inter-tribal war during the 100,000+ years before European contact.

Pre-contact tribes also didn't have one "alpha" chief. They had tribal councils, consisting of elderly men and women whose life experiences were valued. Young physically strong hunters were always expected to show deference to these elders. Among the Lakota, the hunter who made the kill always ate last, reinforcing the virtue of humility and discouraging arrogance. Might was not right in tribal society. The very concept of "chief" was foisted upon native people by the Crown colonizers.

The Luciferian European nobility saw this socialist tribal model as a threat to their growing industrial capitalist empire. So their hired guns led by Albert Pike - founder of both Scottish-Rite Freemasonry in the US and the Ku Klux Klan - launched the Indian Wars.

These mercenaries also taught Indians to collect scalps, paying them a bounty before sending the scalps back to the Euro-inbreds who did God knows what with them. The Crown Agent Skull & Bones Society reportedly keeps Geronimo's skull in its Yale University house of horrors.

Pike's troops then hand-picked tribal "chiefs" of low character that were easily bought - usually with whiskey. These "chiefs" replaced the traditional tribal councils, signed treaties giving away tribal land, and were bribed into attacking other tribes to create the disunity necessary for the Illuminati to destroy the Native American nature-based model of living with the earth instead of pilfering it.

Pike was a 33rd degree Mason and Crown Agent. He brought Freemasonry to America at Charleston, SC in the 1870's. His book *Morals and Dogma* serves as a bible for US Freemasons today. In the book Pike proclaims the Satanic bent of Freemasonry espousing, "The Masonic Religion should be by all of us initiates in the High Degrees maintained in the purity of the Luciferic Doctrine".

Neo-Darwinism is a diabolical, fear-laden Luciferian way of thinking about the world. It is a reality at odds with nature. The dominance paradigm it justifies is a Western industrial human construct conjured up as a rationale for past, present and future subjugation of the planet and its people by the Illuminati bloodline elite.

One last thought: If control over the global economy really is as simple as "survival of the fittest" and "alpha male dominance", shouldn't Evander Holyfield own Bank of America, while Goldman Sachs' scrawny CEO Lloyd Blankfein rents a cockroach-infested shack in Harlem?

CHAPTER 8

PSYCHOLOGICAL WARFARE FOR ALL

The inbred Luciferian bloodline elite have, over the centuries, refined the techniques they employ to assure continued dominion over the resources of the planet and its people. In the early days the Crown publicly crucified and tortured rebellious citizens, sprinkling in the occasional bloody peasant massacre when things got dicey. These open displays of barbarism ensured a climate of fear that thwarted any challenge to their hegemony.

The Crown's global terror network still serves this function. If they can kill JFK and pull off 911, they can kill any of us, right? And that's exactly what they want you to internalize as part of their perception management program This perception keeps you full of fear - the language of Satan - rather than full of courage and love - the language of God.

Death and destruction are the bread and butter of the Illuminati business plan. World Wars create the most revenue and the most blood sacrifice, upon which these fallen angels feed.

On August 15, 1871 Sovereign Grand Commander of the Ancient & Accepted Scottish Rite of Freemasonry General Albert Pike, the aforementioned Ku Klux Klan founder and Indian war prosecutor, wrote a letter to Italian P-1 33rd Degree Grand Commander and Mafia founder Guiseppe Mazzini.

In the letter Pike talked of a Brotherhood plan for three World Wars. The first, he said, would destroy czarist Russia and create a Communist "bogeyman" that the bankers could employ to justify their foreign interventions around the world. The second, Pike said, would be used to create Israel, which would become a mercenary force for the international bankers while protecting oil interests in the Middle East for the Rothschild and Rockefeller combines.

The Third World War, stated Pike's letter, would pit Arabs against Zionists, and would culminate in a New World Order completely controlled by the international bankers and their secret societies.

Pike described the events that would unfold as pretext for WWIII, "We must provoke a social cataclysm which in all its horror...everywhere, the citizens obliged to defend themselves against the world minority of revolutionaries...will receive the true light through...the pure doctrine of Lucifer, brought finally out into public view."

While it has been easy for the Crown to pit nation against nation with their agents embedded on both sides, quelling domestic dissent has proven a bit more difficult.

The medieval servitude of the Dark Ages and the ancient gallows employed to deal with dissenters eventually provoked revolution in such disparate locales as France, America and Russia. More recently, the Crown's equally crude, if better armed, corporate sponsored fascist resource-control juntas have produced the same revolutionary result in Iran, Iraq, Syria, Cuba, North Korea, the Congo, Angola, Mozambique, Zimbabwe, Vietnam, Chile, Afghanistan, Nicaragua, El Salvador, Bolivia, Ecuador and Venezuela to name just a few.

Befuddled, the bloodline Babylonians were forced to shift to a more veiled menu of covert assassination, well-funded opposition parties, NGO intrigues, currency counterfeiting, leaflet drops, fake trucker's strikes and all manner of counter-revolutionary shenanigans. But even these deceptions are eventually exposed, especially with the surge in truth journalism on the Internet. Brutality is brutality, however subtle and disguised.

When this strategy failed to stem the tide of history, provoking a democratic and thus subversive reaction among the populace, the international banking syndicate and its coterie of idle rich Luciferians turned to psychological warfare as their mainstay.

They learned that it was much easier to control a population through Tavistock Institute-funded television and Internet brainwashing, than to be forced to mow down a more cognizant citizenry in the streets and risk backlash. The key is to keep people docile, fearful, ignorant and filled with self-hatred.

Another way the Crown steers public opinion is through their Bridge Fund foundations. In 1913 the Rockefeller Foundation came into being. It would shield the Rockefeller's wealth from the coming income tax provisions of the never-ratified 16th Amendment. More importantly it would allow these Federal Reserve (formed the same year) Illuminati owners to steer public opinion through social engineering via grant patronage.

One of the Foundation's most infamous tentacles was the General Education Board. In Occasional Letter #1 the Board stated, "In our dreams we have limitless resources and the people yield themselves with perfect docility to our molding hands. The present education conventions fade from their minds and, unhampered by tradition, we will work our own good will upon a grateful and responsive rural folk. We shall try not to make these people or any of their children into philosophers or men of learning or men of science...of whom we have ample supply."

Over the next decades the condescending financial parasites at Club Fed would fabricate all matter of story lines and staged events to keep the "rural folk" frightened and inert. These included the Great Depression, the Cold War, McCarthyism, the threat of nuclear Armageddon, the Kennedy, Malcom X and Martin Luther King Jr. assassinations and 911. All of these were also, quite conveniently, financial boons for the international banking syndicate and their defense/oil/drug mafia cartels.

The current "scary story lines" include school shootings, Ebola virus and Muslim extremism. All are problem-reaction-solution contrivances of the Crown and its tentacles. The latter is central to my book, *Big Oil & Their Bankers in the Persian Gulf: Four Horsemen, Eight Families & Their Global Intelligence, Narcotics & Terror Network.*

All of these terrors are created for specific reasons as part of the bigger agenda being slowly pushed forward by the Luciferians behind the Crown. The Freemason *modus operandi* is *Order Ab Chao* - Order out of Chaos.

Centered in Pakistan the Crown-subsidiary Agha Khan Foundation is funded by the Illuminati's secret Muslim Brotherhood society. It churns out "Muslim extremists" who are then "handled" by the Cabalistic Rothschild intelligence arm, which is more commonly known as the Israeli Mossad.

These "Muslim extremists" are then used to butcher local resistance while the bankers grab the oilfields in whichever Middle East country they find it in. The Afghan opium monopoly was achieved in the very same way, along with the recently opened natural gas pipeline from Turkmenistan to the Pakistani port of Karachi.

911 was the well-contrived scheme used to launch the phony war on terror and its parallel permanent war economy that lit up Wall Street banks and their war profiteer cartels like Christmas trees. Pearl Harbor served the same purpose in justifying US entry in defense of the Crown in WWII.

Despite their attempts to hard-wire their lies into us via the Internet and TV, for many the scary bedtime stories are wearing off. Despite the constant stream of lies emanating from the Tavistock media wing of the Illuminati banksters, millions of people around the world are waking up.

As Pete Townsend of The Who sang, the important thing now is that we "Don't Get Fooled Again." Because as their plan moves into a new phase, the tools at their disposal are integrating. Technology is the key. And these new systems involve low-frequency weaponry capable of creating alien (AI) perceptions or "virtual realities" in human consciousness which are much more amenable to the furtherance of the Luciferian agenda.

PART II

THE LUCIFERIAN AGENDA

CHAPTER 9

AGENDA 21

In 1992, just as the US Democratic Party was being hijacked by the Illuminati Presidency of Bill Clinton, and just as the UK Labor Party was about to be surrendered to Illuminati Prime Minister Tony Blair, there was a meeting in Rio de Janeiro that would, under the soft fuzzy guise of "sustainability", implement the Luciferian plan to end humanity.

With anything resembling an organized left wing political opposition to their global fascist plan knocked out by the rise of the right-leaning Clinton and Blair - and the subsequent surrender of their respective long-standing worker parties to the bankers - the Satanists would now use the constituents of these two parties to help manufacture a crisis through which they could justify total control over the planet.

The *Order Ab Chao* pretext was environmental cataclysm and global warming. Both Democrats and Labor took the bait, as did many well-meaning people around the world who knew through observation that there was something seriously wrong with the weather, but could never imagine it being used to further the agenda of the Illuminati.

With Occidental Petroleum billionaire owner Armand Hammer's protege Al Gore as its spokesman, the Luciferians would now promote their myth of scarcity, which assigns blame to humanity instead of to themselves. From their Babylonian pulpit they preached misanthropy, carbon footprints, carbon taxes, tiny houses, a contraction in living standards and general austerity.

All the while, Illuminati puppets Clinton and Blair were busy deregulating the banks of Glass-Steagall, merging corporations, privatizing education, increasing killer vaccinations, rolling out glycophosphates and GMO foods, launching a low-frequency weapons war via the introduction of the Internet and polluting entire ecosystems with their Eight Families cartels.

But we were not to blame the elites. We were to blame ourselves and our fellow humans. In fact, we were to think that "humans" had screwed up the planet so badly that the world would be better off without us. The ultimate self-hatred was becoming a normalized plank in their perception management offensive.

Environmental groups led the charge, their boards filled with Crown agents, bankers and corporate oil, mining and chemical CEOs. Prince Charles spearheaded much of the public relations, Prince Albert led the anti-human mantras.

In Rio de Janeiro, it was the Honorable Maurice Strong pulling the anti-humanity bandwagon. Strong is a Canadian oil and mining billionaire who once suggested, "Isn't the only hope for the planet that the industrialized civilizations collapse? Isn't it our responsibility to bring that about?"

Out of this June 1992 Rio Earth Summit came a human control plan that came to be known as Agenda 21. Some of its goals include an end to national sovereignty, the restructuring of the family unit, the assignment of certain jobs for certain people, restrictions of people's movements, an increase in the role of the state in raising children, the creation of densely populated human settlement zones accompanied by an emptying out of rural areas, a dumbing down of education via testing rather than learning, the abolition of private property, and at its core a massive reduction in the population of Planet Earth.

Under the guise of a front called Local Governments for Sustainability, the elitist polluters have set out to push this anti-human agenda into every corner of the planet. The word "sustainability" is their Trojan Horse. Wherever you see it used, know that it has nothing to do with protecting the earth, and everything to do with destroying it and you.

Using the typical inverted morality of Lucifer, these pigs who have trashed this planet, now seek to make us feel culpable for their crimes via the guilt and shame-ridden "environmental movement". It's the perfect cover for the evil agenda they have planned for us.

The key to their plan is depopulation. The Georgia Guide Stones, which no one seems to know who built, call for the population of earth to be maintained under 500,000 million. The stones are astrologically aligned and the writing is in several languages, some of them ancient.

A separate draft copy of the United Nations Global Biodiversity Assessment calls for a population of 1 billion. This would also be a massive cull since the current world population is around 7.6 billion.

Using 911 as yet another pretext, the Illuminati have embarked on a plan of permanent war economy, first justified by the fake war on terror. While their Crown Agent companies and banks get the arms, oil, aid and rebuilding contracts, they are also using this model to achieve their goal of global depopulation.

CHAPTER 10

THE ILLUMINATI DEPOPULATION AGENDA

While the global elite construct underground bunkers, eat organic food, and hoard seeds in Arctic vaults; the global poor are being slowly starved thanks to high commodity prices and poisoned with genetically modified (GMO) food.

Austerity measures aimed largely at the poor are being imposed on all the nations of the world through the Illuminati IMF. Weather events grow more deadly and brush fire wars more frequent. An AK-47 can be obtained for $49 in the markets of West Africa. The depopulation campaign of the inbred Illuminati bankers is accelerating.

In 1957 President Dwight Eisenhower, who later warned of a "military-industrial complex", commissioned a panel of scientists to study the issue of overpopulation. The scientists put forth Alternatives I, II and III, advocating both the release of deadly viruses and perpetual warfare as means to decrease world population.

The first supposition dovetailed nicely with the pharmaceutical interests of the Rockefellers. According to Nexus magazine, the Rockefellers own one-half of the US pharmaceutical industry, which will reap billions developing medicines and vaccines to "battle" the deadly viruses about to be released.

In 1969 the Senate Church Committee discovered that the US Defense Department (DOD) had requested a budget of tens of millions of taxpayer dollars for a program to speed development of new viruses that target and destroy the human immune system.

DOD officials testified before Congress that they planned to produce, "a synthetic biological agent, an agent that does not naturally exist and for which no natural immunity could be acquired...Most important is that it might be refractory to the immunological and therapeutic processes upon which we depend to maintain our relative freedom from infectious disease."

House Bill 5090 authorized the funds and MK-NAOMI was carried out at Fort Detrick, Maryland. Out of this research came the AIDS virus, which was targeted at "undesirable elements" of the population. The first AIDS viruses were administered through a massive smallpox vaccine campaign in central and southern Africa by the World Health Organization in 1977. A year later ads appeared in major US newspapers soliciting "promiscuous gay male volunteers" to take part in a Hepatitis B vaccine study.

The program targeted male homosexuals age 20-40 in New York City, Los Angeles, Chicago, St. Louis and San Francisco. It was administered by the US Centers for Disease Control which, under its earlier incarnation as the US Public Health Department in Atlanta, oversaw the Tuskegee syphilis experiments on African American males.

San Francisco has been a target of numerous CIA experiments, due to its high population of left-leaning citizens, which the Illuminati views as "undesirables". According to Dr. Eva Snead, San Francisco has one of the highest cancer rates in the country.

For years Malathion, first developed by the Nazis, was sprayed over the city by helicopters from CIA Evergreen Air, whose Arizona base was used, according to author William Cooper, as a CIA transshipment point for Colombian cocaine. The mysterious Legionnaire's Disease occurs often in San Francisco and the CIA's MK-ULTRA mind control bad acid program was based there.

The intellectual force behind the introduction of AIDS was the Bilderberger Group, which became fixated on population control after WWII. William Cooper said that the Policy Committee of the Bilderbergers gave orders to DOD to introduce the AIDS virus. The Bilderbergers are close to the Club of Rome, which was founded on a Rockefeller estate near Bellagio, Italy and is backed by the same European Black Nobility who frequent Bilderberger meetings.

A 1968 study by the Club of Rome advocated lowering the birth rate and increasing the death rate. Club founder Dr. Aurelio Peccei made a top-secret recommendation to introduce a microbe that would attack the auto-immune system, then develop a vaccine as a prophylactic for the global elite.

One month after the 1968 Club of Rome meeting Paul Ehrlich published The Population Bomb. The book hints at a draconian depopulation plan in the works. On page seventeen Ehrlich writes, "The problem could have been avoided by population control...so that a 'death rate solution' did not have to occur." A year later MK-NAOMI was born.

Peccei himself authored the Club of Rome's much-touted Global 2000 report, which President Jimmy Carter pushed on his BCCI shakedown cruise of Africa. Peccei wrote in the report, "Man is now vested with unprecedented, tremendous responsibilities and thrown into the role of moderator of life on the planet, including his own"

The Bilderbergers were behind the Haig-Kissinger Depopulation Policy, a driving force at the State Department and administered by the National Security Council. Pressure was applied to Third World countries to reduce their populations. Those that did not comply saw their US aid withheld or were subject to Pink Plan low-intensity war that targets civilians, especially women of child-bearing age.

In Africa famine and brush-fire wars are encouraged. AK-47 rifles can be bought at West African markets for under $50. The same is true in the markets of Peshawar, Pakistan. In 1975, a year after attending a Club of Rome conference on the topic, Secretary of State and Crown Agent Henry Kissinger founded the Office of Population Affairs (OPA).

Latin American OPA case officer Thomas Ferguson spilled the beans on OPA's agenda when he stated, "There is a single theme behind all our work; we must reduce population levels. Either they do it our way, through nice clean methods or they will get the kind of mess that we have in El Salvador, or in Iran, or in Beirut...Once population is out of control it requires authoritarian government, even fascism, to reduce it...The professionals aren't interested in reducing population for humanitarian reasons...Civil wars are somewhat drawn-out ways to reduce population. The quickest way to reduce population is through famine like in Africa. We go into a country and say, here is your goddamn development plan. Throw it out the window. Start looking at your population...if you don't ... then you'll have an El Salvador or an Iran, or worse, a Cambodia".

Ferguson said of El Salvador, "To accomplish what the State Department deems adequate population control, the civil war (run by CIA) would have to be greatly expanded. You have to pull all the males into fighting and kill significant numbers of fertile, child-bearing age females. You are killing a small number of males and not enough fertile females to do the job...If the war went on 30-40 years, you might accomplish something. Unfortunately, we don't have too many instances of this to study".

Report from Iron Mountain

In 1961 Kennedy Administration officials McGeorge Bundy, Robert McNamara and Dean Rusk, all CFR and Bilderberger members, led a study group that looked into "the problem of peace". The group met at Iron Mountain, a huge underground corporate nuclear shelter near Hudson, New York, where CFR think tank The Hudson Institute is located. The bunker contains redundant offices in case of nuclear attack for Exxon Mobil, Royal Dutch/Shell and JP Morgan Chase. A copy of the group discussions, known as Report from Iron Mountain, was leaked by a participant and published in 1967 by Dial Press.

The report's authors saw war as necessary and desirable stating "War itself is the basic social system, within which other secondary modes of social organization conflict or conspire. (War is) the principal organizing force...the essential economic stabilizer of modern societies." The group worried that through "ambiguous leadership" the "ruling administrative class" might lose its ability to "rationalize a desired war", leading to the "actual disestablishment of military institutions".

The report goes on to say, "...the war system cannot responsibly be allowed to disappear until...we know exactly what we plan to put in its place...The possibility of war provides the sense of external necessity without which no government can long remain in power...The basic authority of a modern state over its people resides in its war powers. War has served as the last great safeguard against the elimination of necessary classes."

Historian Howard Zinn described this conundrum when he wrote, "American capitalism needed international rivalry - and periodic war - to create an artificial community of interest between rich and poor, supplanting the genuine community of interest among the poor that showed itself in sporadic movements".

The Iron Mountain gang was not the first to discover the virtues of war. In 1909 the trustees of the Andrew Carnegie Foundation for International Peace met to discuss pre-WWI American life. Many of the participants were members of Skull and Bones. They concluded, "There are no known means more efficient than war, assuming the objective is altering the life of an entire people...How do we involve the United States in a war?"

The Report from Iron Mountain goes on to propose a proper role for those of the lower classes, crediting military institutions with providing "antisocial elements with an acceptable role in the social structure. The younger and more dangerous of these hostile social groupings have been kept under control by the Selective Service System...A possible surrogate for the control of potential enemies of society is the reintroduction, in some form consistent with modern technology and political process, of slavery...The development of a sophisticated form of slavery may be an absolute prerequisite for social control in a world at peace."

The Iron Mountain goons, though thrilled by the idea of slavery, listed as other socioeconomic substitutions for war: a comprehensive social welfare program, a giant open-ended space program aimed at unreachable targets, a permanent arms inspection regime, an omnipresent global police and peacekeeping force, massive global environmental pollution that would require a large labor pool to clean up, socially-oriented blood sports, and a comprehensive eugenics program.

The 1990 Gulf War genocide fulfilled the dreams of the Club of Rome Zero Population Growth maniacs, while also providing a testing ground for two of the war substitutes proposed by the Iron Mountain fascists: an arms inspection regime and UN peacekeepers. Both concepts gained traction in the international community thanks to the Gulf War.

Let the Iraqi Genocide Begin

Estimates of Iraqi casualties during the Gulf War are sobering. Some organizations like Greenpeace put the death toll at near one million people. It was a war in which the media was denied access on a scale never before seen, so casualty figures vary greatly. According to Tony Murphy, a researcher at the International War Crimes Tribunal, the US attack on Iraq killed 125,000 civilians, while destroying 676 schools, 38 hospitals, 8 major hydroelectric dams, 11 power plants, 119 power substations and half the country's telephone lines. The attacks occurred mostly at night when people were most vulnerable.

In the months following the war the death rate of Iraqi children under five tripled. Thirty-eight percent of these deaths were caused by diarrhea. Victor Filatov, a Russian journalist reporting for Sovetskaya Rossiya from post-war Baghdad wrote, "What further bloodshed do these barbarians of the 20th century need? I thought the Americans had changed since Vietnam...but no, they never change. They remain true to themselves."

According to former US Attorney General Ramsey Clark, the US was found guilty of nineteen war crimes against Iraq before the

International War Crimes Tribunal. The US dropped 88,000 tons of bombs on Iraq during the Gulf War and has rained down countless more bombs since. Many bombs were tipped with armor piercing depleted uranium (DU) warheads, which may account for chronic Iraqi health problems.

Dr. Siegwart-Horst Gunther, a German physician who came to Iraq to help its people, became gravely ill when he handled just one cigar-sized fragment from a DU warhead. Dr. Gunther measured the tiny object's radioactivity to be 11 microSv per hour, whereas an acceptable exposure is no more than 300 microSv per year. Three hundred tons of DU ammunition was deployed during the war.

Many believe DU is responsible for Gulf War Syndrome, which has killed and permanently injured many US soldiers who fought in the Persian Gulf theater. Since 2000, nearly 11,000 US Gulf War veterans have died from Gulf War Syndrome, while the Pentagon continues to cover up this travesty.

Satanism and Psychotronic Warfare

The US also tested numerous top-secret high-tech weapons systems in the Gulf theater, while utilizing some old low-frequency favorites. When Iraqi ground forces surrendered, many of them were in a state of delirium and lethargy that could have been induced by extremely low-frequency radio waves, which the US used as a weapon as early as the Vietnam conflict.

Yale University and CIA psychiatrist Dr. Jose Delgado studied mind control for the Company during the 1950's as part of the MK-ULTRA program. Delgado determined, "Physical control of many brain functions is a demonstrated fact...it is even possible to create and follow intentions...By electronic stimulation of specific cerebral structures, movements can be induced by radio command...by remote control."

According to a military document written by Colonel Paul Valley and Major Michael Aquino titled From PSYOP to Mindwar: The Psychology of Victory, the US Army used an operational weapons system "to map the minds of neutral and enemy individuals and then to change them in accordance with US national interests".

The technique was used to secure the surrender of 29,276 armed Viet Cong and North Vietnamese Army soldiers in 1967 and 1968. The US Navy was also heavily involved in "psychotronic" research. Many US soldiers who served near the DMZ that divided North and South Vietnam claimed to see UFOs on a regular basis. The Pentagon Papers revealed that an electronic barrier was placed along the DMZ by the secretive JASON Society.

Major Michael Aquino was an Army psyops specialist in Vietnam, where his unit specialized in drug-inducement, brainwashing, virus injection, brain implants, hypnosis, and use of electromagnetic fields and extremely low-frequency radio waves.

After Vietnam, Aquino moved to San Francisco and founded the Temple of Set. Set is the ancient Egyptian name for Lucifer. Aquino was now a senior US Military Intelligence official. He'd been given a Top Secret security clearance on June, 9, 1981. Less than a month later an Army intelligence memo revealed that Aquino's Temple of Set was an off-shoot of Anton LaVey's Church of Satan, also headquartered in San Francisco. Two other Set members were Willie Browning and Dennis Mann. Both were Army Intelligence officers.

The Temple of Set was obsessed with military matters and political fascism. It was especially preoccupied with the Nazi Order of the Trapezoid. Aquino's "official" job was history professor at Golden Gate College. The Temple recruited the same Hells Angels who Billy Mellon Hitchcock had used to dole out his bad CIA acid. Its members frequented prostitutes where they engaged in all manner of sadomasochistic activities. Director of Army Counter-Intelligence Donald Press revealed that Dennis Mann was assigned to the 306 PSYOPS Battalion and that Aquino was assigned to a top secret program known as Presidio.

Presidio is also the name of a spooky complex in the Golden Gate National Recreation Area, which Mikhail Gorbachev reportedly frequented as the Soviet Union was falling apart. Was Aquino part of an operation to "map the mind" of the Soviet Union's last leader and induce him into proposing both glasnost and perestroika, the two free market policies that ultimately led to the Soviet Union's demise? Remember the curious mark that suddenly appeared on Gorbachev's forehead? Was he implanted with some sort of microchip mind-control device to make him think "in accordance with US national interests"?

Such Orwellian technology is marketed on a regular basis throughout the world. International Healthline Corporation and others sell microchip implants in the US, Russia and Europe. The Humane Society has adopted a policy of micro-chipping all stray pets. The State of Hawaii requires that all pets be micro-chipped.

Six thousand people in Sweden have accepted a microchip in their hand that they use for all purchases. Trials are also underway in Japan. In July 2002, National Public Radio reported a similar trial beginning in Seattle. Later in 2002, after a rash of suspicious abductions of young girls, BBC reported that a British company plans to implant children with microchips so that their parents can monitor their whereabouts. In 2017, a Wisconsin company micro-chipped its employees. That same year the drug Abilify was chipped.

Dr. Carl Sanders, a highly acclaimed electronics engineer, revealed that a microchip project he launched to help people with severed spinal cords was taken over by the Bill Colby's Operation Phoenix in a series of meetings organized by Henry Kissinger. Sanders says the optimal spot for a microchip implant is just below the hairline on a person's forehead, since the device can be recharged by changes in body temperatures, which are most pronounced there. Interestingly, this is the location of the pineal gland or Third Eye.

The 1986 Emigration Control Act grants the President the power to mandate any kind of ID he deems necessary. Researchers at Southern California have developed a chip that mimics the hippocampus, the part of the brain that deals with memory. Pentagon officials are interested in using it in experiments to create a "super-soldier". Another microchip called Braingate is being implanted in paralyzed people. It allows them to control their environment by simply thinking.

In Iraq, psychological warfare gave way to slow genocide. According to UNICEF, as of late 2001, 1.5 million Iraqi children had died as a result of sanctions, while one child in ten died before their first birthday. Thalassemia, anemia and diarrhea were the biggest killers and could have been prevented were it not for a chronic shortage of blood and medicine in Iraq due to the sanctions. UN Committee 661 served as arbiter of what constituted a "dual use" item and therefore banned for import into Iraq. As of 2001, over 1,600 Iraqi contracts with Western companies for medical equipment had been blocked by 661.

The Gulf War decimated Iraq's sewer and water treatment systems. Iraqis were forced to drink polluted water, leading to numerous health problems. Iraq was not allowed to import chlorine to clean the water since 661 deemed it a potential chemical weapon. Electrical power was rationed in three-hour daily increments per household since the Iraqi government couldn't get the parts it needed to fix its power plants after the US bombed its entire power grid. With the devaluation of the Iraqi dinar and the ban on the export of 2.4 million barrels of oil per day, the average Iraqi lived on $2.50 a month - enough to buy a pair of shoes. The only Iraqis not affected were the wealthy elite, who had long ago stashed their savings overseas in US dollars.

UNICEF estimates that 28% of Iraqi children no longer went to school. Before the war almost all children attended. Often families could only afford to send one child to school because of the cost of simple things like backpacks, shoes and notebooks. Rafah Salam Aziz, Director of Mansour Children's Hospital, said parents were often forced to make similar decisions about their children's lives. Aziz said, "Many times it's easier for a family to let a baby die rather than let the whole family go hungry and get sick."

But depopulation is just part of the reason that the Illuminati finance the permanent war economy. As former Dutch banker and Illuminati defector Ronald Bernard tells us, war is also part of the Masonic project to provide a steady blood sacrifice on which the Luciferians feed to increase their power.

Bernard says that our birth certificate places each of us into a bondage to the Satanists. In the corporation called Holland for example, a baby is assigned a debt of five-hundred thousand euros. Throughout their life each person, through a series of taxes, consumption and wage slavery, is expected to pay back this debt to the Illuminati. In many countries birth certificates are traded on the stock exchanges.

Since we slaves have already built out their infrastructure, these freaks now wish to depopulate 90% of humanity, but they have a plan for the rest of us as well.

The end game of the Masonic project, Bernard says, is to turn us all into batteries to generate the negative energy that, along with wars and outright human sacrifice, fuels the 4th dimension evil consciousness.

Trans-humanism plays a big part in this agenda, since they have to convince us that we have no souls and are only machines. Trans-genderism is a stepping stone towards this goal. This accounts for many recent popular movies promoting trans-humanism. The Tavistock Institute is behind these movies through their Hofjuden Hollywood cartel.

Soon Alexa will not only be recording your conversations and sending them to the authorities, as happened recently to an Oregon couple. It will also be programming your thoughts, turning you into a miserable blithering idiot, whose unhappiness and confusion is rocket fuel for the Illuminati.

But there are many other ways in which the Babylonian priesthood keeps us dumbed down, unhealthy and unaware of both our own immense powers and of their criminal agenda.

CHAPTER 11

TOXIC FOOD FOR THE MASSES

There is a lot of talk these days about being prepared for natural and man-made disasters. Finding classes, lectures, videos and books on how to be self-sufficient is as simple as a click of the mouse. Some people even scoff at preppers, saying they are overly paranoid. However, if you consider the staggering number of deep-earth bunkers that have been constructed for the military and super-elite, and those still under construction, you might think twice about becoming a prepper yourself. Just the idea of it should make the rational mind wonder. If the gendarme branches and their upper-class handlers are so fixated with survival bunkers fortified with everything needed to live comfortably for 50-75 years, maybe shit really is about to hit the fan.

Indeed, how can anyone sit back in comfort after witnessing the massive disasters that unfolded during hurricanes Katrina, Harvey, and Irma. What of the 2017 California wildfires, the massive earthquakes in Mexico, or the eruption of Hawaii's Kilauea volcano? Among the myriads of man-made world-wide disasters that many of us see coming down the road, there is one of epic proportions that is currently underway – yet, too few have yet to recognize it.

By now, the entire world population has heard of GMOs or Genetically Modified Organisms, but apparently not everyone understands exactly what these are or what they mean to the average person. The World Health Organization describes them as "...organisms in which the genetic material (DNA) has been altered in a way that does not occur naturally. The technology is referred to as "modern biotechnology", "gene technology", "recombinant DNA technology", or just plain old "genetic engineering". Whatever you want to call it, genetic manipulation allows selected genes to be taken from one organism and forced into another.

It is important to realize that the genes used to develop GMO plants and food crops can and often do belong to any number of living organisms, including unrelated plants, animals, insects, bacteria, viruses, fungi, and even human genes.

People who have a deep and abiding faith in a Creator God of any kind should be especially horrified at this Island of Dr. Moreau experiment on the human population. If God had intended rice and mice to splice mad scientists wouldn't have to force DNA from one species into another using viruses as a vector - it would happen naturally.

While I certainly don't intend to eat any mice in the near future, nearly half of the world's population relies on rice as a staple food source. Until there is a real law that requires the listing of GMO ingredients we cannot trust that the food we buy in the grocery stores aren't made with a mutant strain of monkey virus or worse.

There are very real concerns as to how genetically modified foods act upon the human and animal body. Not only were the big bio-tech companies allowed free reign to play God with our food, they also got to carry out and present their own research to the FDA and USDA to "prove" that GMO foods and their associated herbicides and pesticides were safe for human consumption. The Big 6 Franken-Food purveyors are BASF, Bayer, DuPont, Dow Chemical Company, Monsanto, and Syngenta.

The wolf in sheep's clothing is guarding the pasture, and if you want to eat or farm or sell seed, you had better get on board or be prepared to be lied to, coerced, or run out of business.

The powerful lobby of these chemical companies, who brought the world delights such as Agent Orange and DDT, are granted all manner of privileges by cowardly government officials who don't dare confront them.

Among the many free passes given to these almighty chemical companies include the acceptance of laughable in-house research studies that are clearly manipulated either by their own lackey scientists or by bought-off labs and universities to raise little, if any cause for alarm.

In fact, long before the FDA was cow-towed by the powerful hammer of Monsanto, their own scientists repeatedly warned that GM foods might create unpredictable and hard-to-detect side effects, such as increasing food allergies, a build up of toxins in the body, newly emerging diseases and "conditions", a worsening of existing diseases and syndromes, nutritional problems, and serious digestive disorders such as leaky gut syndrome - a precursor to celiac and other digestive disorders.

Yet, even as long-term safety studies of GMO crops were being called for by the FDA, reports of their detrimental impacts were already flooding in.

In India, thousands of sheep, buffalo, and goats died after grazing on Round-Up Ready Bt cotton plants. Mice that ate GM corn had fewer and smaller babies and exhibited signs of aggression, confusion and unsocial behavior - the same behaviors found in the human disease Autism.

Additional studies demonstrated that more than half of the babies born to mother rats that were fed GM soy, died within three weeks. Hamsters that were fed GM soy lost the ability to have babies by the third generation. Rodents fed GM corn and soy showed immune system dysfunction and signs of toxicity.

The stomach lining of rats fed GM potatoes showed excessive cell growth, a condition that may lead to cancer. One study on animals that ate GM food found that they developed organ lesions, altered liver and pancreas cells, changed enzyme levels, and many other disturbing effects. All these studies and more were done in the early GMO years.

Even the American Academy of Environmental Medicine (AAEM) reports, "…several animal studies indicate serious health risks associated with GM food consumption including infertility, immune dysregulation, accelerated aging, dysregulation of genes associated with cholesterol synthesis, insulin regulation, cell signaling, and protein formation, and changes in the liver, kidney, spleen and gastrointestinal system."

The AAEM was so disturbed by their studies that they took an important and historically significant stand by asking physicians to advise their patients to avoid GM foods.

It is quite apparent that there is more than a casual association between GM foods and adverse health effects. Increasingly, genetically modified foods are being blamed for sudden increases in incidences of autism and Alzheimer's disease in areas where they were recently introduced into the food system.

In the UK, soy allergies skyrocketed by 50% soon after GM soy was introduced. And for those who are allergic to soy, you should know that cooked GM soy protein contains as much as seven-times the amount of known allergens as compared to non-GM soy.

In the early GMO years these Franken-Food murderers were promising to feed the world while at the same time twisting the arms of any farmer who resisted planting their seed. And any truly independent researcher daring to investigate or study the claims made by one of these Big 6 Franken-Food companies was quashed as ruthlessly and effectively as an insect doused with Monsanto's DDT.

Despite their ruthless tactics, many truly independent studies were able to be conducted outside of the long reach of Monsanto and Friends, and they turned up some truly frightening results.

In September of 2012 a two-year peer-reviewed study on the effects of feeding Monsanto's NK603 GMO Roundup Ready corn to rats and exposing them to exceedingly low levels of Roundup herbicide was published by researchers at Caen University in France. Their findings found seriously alarming results that indicated the dangers of GM food, feed, and their associated herbicides.

The study was based on the same exact protocols Monsanto had used in 2004 to prove that their corn was safe for consumption. But the scientists in the Caen study increased the length of the research period from Monsanto's paltry 90-day study to a more revealing 2-year study. The Caen scientists also wanted more documentation as to the effects of their study, so they not only increased the number of animals tested (it was already the largest animal study of its kind) but increased the frequency of testing and the number of factors that would be tested for.

Researchers tested for three doses (rather than two in the usual ninety-day long protocols) of the Roundup-tolerant NK603 GMO maize alone, the GMO maize treated with Roundup, and Roundup alone at very low environmentally relevant doses starting below the range of levels permitted by regulatory authorities in drinking water and in GM feed." What they found was nothing short of horrific.

It took only four months (eight weeks more than the Monsanto-led study) for the research team to begin seeing the negative physical effects. The Caen study rats developed 400 times the number of large tumors and died 2-3 times more often - and faster - than the control group. They had increased mammary tumors, affected pituitary glands, and congestion and necrosis of the liver. Researches also found that exceedingly low doses of Roundup disrupted estrogen and androgen receptors in cells and acted as a sexual endocrine disruptor in live animals.

According to the study, "By the beginning of the 24th month, 50–80% of female animals had developed tumors in all treated groups, with up to three tumors per animal, whereas only 30% of controls [non-GMO-fed] were affected. The Roundup treatment groups showed the greatest rates of tumor incidence with 80% of animals affected with up to three tumors for one female in each group."

Read that again very slowly and imagine that we humans are the rats.

An earlier study conducted in 2011, entitled,"Maternal and fetal exposure to pesticides associated to genetically modified foods in Eastern Townships of Quebec", led by Aziz Aris and Samuel

Leblanc and published in the journal *Reproductive Toxicology*, found Bt toxin and the herbicides glyphosate and gluphosinate in nearly 100% of pregnant (and non-pregnant) women and their unborn babies. And a more recent study of randomly selected participants from around the country had glyphosate (Roundup) in their blood and urine.

A few years ago I might have said to you that only certified organic foods do not contain genetically modified organisms, but I can't say that anymore. That's because we know that GMO plants often have an increased ability to cross-pollinate with their open-pollinated and heirloom counterparts, like corn.

In one early and devastating experiment that took place in 1998, University of Chicago scientists were working on genetically modifying a variety of mustard to be herbicide resistant. And while no known gene effecting floral characteristics was altered in the experiment, the researchers noticed that the flowers from the genetically modified mustard looked different than those on the unaltered mustard. Even though the scientists thought this change was unlikely to be significant, they decided to test the modified plants' out-crossing rate, which essentially tests the speed and effectiveness of pollen moving from the male flower to the female flower in order to produce viable seed.

It turned out that the genetically engineered mustard had over twenty times the out-crossing rate of the standard mustard. In other words, the pollen from the GMO mustard was more than twenty times more likely to successfully reproduce than its natural counterpart in the same scenario. This disturbing fact spells disaster for non-GMO crops grown in the same region as open-pollinated and organic crops, and its outcome has already been felt by farmers all over the Midwest.

Today any and all non-GM open-pollinated heirloom plants are in real danger of being contaminated by their Franken-Food counterparts. This includes natural hybrids, (which are simply a cross of two varieties of a similar species), heirlooms, and open-pollinated vegetables in your garden, as well as seed, grain, cereal, and fruit crops being grown in commercial and organic fields.

And once a non-GMO plant is infected with the patented DNA of a GMO, it is essentially illegal to grow it or save its seed without obtaining legal permission from the patent owner first.

Additionally, multinational corporations like Monsanto are working hard to buy up as many small seed companies as they can in order to gain control of yet more genetic material for their freakish food experiments.

Worse yet, our government has full and complete awareness of the dangers lurking in our food and is doing absolutely nothing to stop it.

In fact many former Monsanto employees now work in positions of power at the FDA and other regulatory agencies that are supposed to monitor the safety of the American food supply. They have the power to approve or deny crops introduced by bio-tech giants like Monsanto, but they choose to climb the ladder of power and enrich themselves and their evil friends rather than save lives.

Even if you have a moral opposition to GMOs, you are probably eating them right now and don't even know it.

That's because there is no law that requires GMO foods and ingredients to be labeled or identified as such. If the laughable labeling bill that was passed a couple of years ago ever goes into effect, there won't be a single word about GMOs on them.

Once again, the onus will be placed on the consumer, who will need to locate and scan a QR Code for every single product they want to buy just to find out if they contain GMOs or not.

The big argument from the GMO-herd is that labeling costs too much (sob). But if the labels have to be changed anyway to include the QR code, why not just print the warning,"This product contains GMOs" and be done with it? Because they know that no one wants to eat Franken-Food, that's why.

The GMO labeling bill also has the organic industry nervous. Democratic Senator Jon Tester told reporters, "...the bill uses a new definition of 'bioengineering' and because USDA is given the authority to determine which foods are considered bioengineered, there could ultimately be a situation where a GMO seed is planted, raised using organic processes, and then certified organic despite it being a GMO plant."

In in July 2018, the Organic Trade Association was called to task for accepting the membership of chemical giant BASF – maker of the deadly dicamba herbicide.- and other non-organic corporate entities and growing modalities, like hydroponics. As the purveyors of chemical and genetic farming worm their way into the lucrative organic market, we may soon see organic food being grown with GMO Franken-seeds and their associated petro-chemicals.

The ruthless and willful contamination of the world's food supply by invasive and irreversible genetic material is the greatest silent disaster in human history. There is absolutely no way to stop the spread of GMOs into our food system and there is no known way to reverse the contamination once it has occurred.

The first solution to this disaster is to educate yourself as to what kinds of GMO ingredients are in the food you buy - which is pretty much everything. Then grill your supermarket manager and local, state, and federal politicians about their stance on GMOs and labeling, and boycott all GMO-foods. If no one buys them, they'll stop growing them.

Better yet, grow and raise as much of your own organic food and seed and animal feed as possible, or buy it directly from a local farmer who does.

CHAPTER 12

POISONING THE ELIXIR

Water has been sacred to mankind since the dawn of time The human body is made up of 75-85% water and without it, life on earth as we know it would end. We are only alive because water is alive. Yet, water all over the world - including the water we drink every single day - is being mindlessly polluted and willfully poisoned. Will this nightmare be the true downfall of mankind?

One of the most wonderful places to appreciate the vast power of water on a physical and spiritual level is from the shore of any great ocean. From that viewpoint, the water seems eternal and ethereal all at the same time. Imagine you are standing on the sun-kissed beaches of California looking out into the reaches of the Pacific Ocean. Travel in your mind across the water for a hundred miles or so and soon you will see the edges of a great island that spans the blue waters as far as an eagle can see.

Welcome to the Great Pacific Garbage Patch (GPGP). First discovered in 1997, this once-living, breathing body of water filled with the most amazing array of life on earth is being choked to death by mankind's *laissez-faire* consumer mentality. This horrific scene is manifested in a swirling gyre of life-sucking garbage and micro-plastic twice the size of Texas and growing every day.

The GPGP was the biggest garbage patch until just recently, when a new floating dump upwards of a million square miles in size – bigger than the country of Mexico - was found in the South Pacific. Those who have seen these monstrosities up close are utterly horrified because they know that what they see floating on top of the water pales in comparison to what lurks just beneath and that which lays in a tangled, life-choking mass on the ocean floor.

As appalling as it is, these vast stretches of ocean trash are but a visual manifestation of the total disregard for the natural world, and water in particular. These garbage patches not only represent obscene consumerism but also industrial greed.

Not only do corporate entities not care about the welfare of nature, they use it intentionally to sabotage the human race in their quest for wealth, power, and control. By destroying water with garbage, sewage, and hazardous waste, they also destroy one of the most fundamental elements of human life, energy, and solace.

The clean water our grandparents took for granted just a few short decades ago is now in serious peril. Rivers, lakes, streams, and oceans carry the bulk of the world's toxic waste. The very rain that falls from the sky is contaminated with industrial toxins, heavy metals, and a whole host of other life-sucking chemicals.

Even the water from public municipal sources - once touted as the cleanest drinking water in the world - is no longer fit for drinking, much less bathing or watering your garden or the commercial crops we rely on for sustenance.

Never mind fecal matter in the water, these days we should be more concerned with industrial pollutants, urban and rural runoff and a frightening array of pharmaceutical drugs in the billions of gallons of feces and urine that are flushed down the toilets of millions of Americans every single day. These and many other toxic substances are increasingly difficult to remove using the water purification systems employed throughout the Western world today. And just imagine those countries that don't have such sophisticated systems.

As if all this weren't bad enough, we also have to contend with pollutants and pharmaceuticals like fluoride and chlorine that are intentionally added to our water after it has been through the purification systems and before it is sent to our water taps.

Chlorine is nasty stuff, but at least it is fairly easy to filter out or allow to evaporate before drinking. On the other hand, fluoride and other pharmaceuticals are extremely difficult to remove.

It's hard to believe that in this day and age that fluoride, an FDA-approved drug first introduced to drinking water in the 1940's, is still being added to municipal water systems around the world. This crime against humanity was based on a lie of epic proportions and it's high time to expose the perpetrators and take control of our water and make it whole again.

It is well known that pre-farming cultures had very little if any dental decay due to a whole food diet that did not include a lot of sugary and floury foods, which cling to teeth and create a cavity-producing bio-film that is very hard to remove with brushing.

This simple fact is proof that humans, along with the rest of the animal world, were created with decay-resistant teeth. Today, both human and animal diets are filled with sticky foods, which not only cause oral decay but are detrimental to overall health. Cavities were pervasive in the colonial and post-colonization era because Europeans simply didn't understand the connection between hygiene and disease. That tradition carried on into the new world for at least a hundred years, if not more before they got clued in.

Fluoride was first introduced to the municipal water supply of the United States in 1945. Government scientists bamboozled the American people into believing that treating the water with fluoride would strengthen tooth enamel and help prevent cavities by up to 65%.

Since then, thousands of in-depth studies have proven beyond a doubt that fluoride does not prevent cavities or protect the teeth in any way. In fact, the World Health Organization has said outright that there is no difference at all in the incidence of tooth decay between the few countries that fluoridate their water and the majority of the world that does not.

Not only is the addition of fluoride to drinking water ineffective, a massive body of evidence exists that proves that fluoride is extremely dangerous to human health, too. At the very minimum, consumption of fluoride in water has been shown to causes irreversible dental fluorosis, which now affects 32% of American children. This drug-induced condition permanently yellows, spots, and rots teeth starting at a very young age. Additionally, accumulation of fluoride in the bones and joints causes skeletal fluorosis, which is a permanent and incredibly painful condition that leads to severe arthritis, bone diseases, and bone cancer.

Fluoride is also known to affect the brain, particularly in the early developmental years of childhood. Not only is the damage compounded over a lifetime of exposure to fluoride, but damage at all levels is permanent. The Illuminati's Agenda 21 ensures that fluoride is added to water to sedate and impede the mental capacity of the masses. The key to avoiding becoming a fluoride zombie is to know the facts. Naturally-occurring fluoride is a mineral called calcium fluoride. It is found in very small amounts in certain types of rocks and in the soils and water they are associated with.

On the other hand, the types of fluoride used in the dentist's office, ADA approved toothpastes and mouthwashes, and in water fluoridation are sodium fluoride, sodium silicofluoride, and fluorosilicic acid (aka hexafluorosilicic acid). All of these types of fluoride are extremely toxic USDA certified pharmaceutical drugs that do not occur in nature anywhere.

The fluoride found in dental products and drinking water are hazardous wastes generated during the manufacturing of steel and aluminum, chemical fertilizers, and nuclear weapons. Aside from their inherent toxicity, they are further contaminated with a whole host of life-sucking poisons including aluminum, lead, and arsenic. Actually, the US government's own toxicity scale lists fluoride as being just slightly less deadly than arsenic.

To give you an idea of the poisonous nature of fluoride, most of the old smelter sites where this garbage first came from are now abandoned Superfund Sites polluted with the very chemicals they are now putting in our water. Additionally, the vast majority of these fluorides are imported to the U.S. from China - a country not known for the quality of its environmental and manufacturing ethics.

Brainwashed proponents of fluoridation, primarily those in the incredibly lucrative dental industry, continue to repeat the Illuminati mantra like a broken record: "Fluoride is a harmless mineral that naturally occurs in water, soil, and food." Blah, blah, blah. The undeniable truth is that these people are even more brainwashed than the general public because they've been deeply indoctrinated into The Society by the "higher education system" to tow the Illuminati agenda.

It's curious to note that fluoride is a drug that requires a prescription to obtain. On every package of ADA and FDA-approved toothpaste and mouthwash is a warning not to swallow the product. If you do, you are advised to call the Poison Control Center. Yet, this drug is freely administered for consumption in municipal water systems in the US and many other countries.

The toxic dose of toothpaste for which it is advised to seek medical attention is about the size of a pea. Yet the equivalent amount of fluoride is found in every 8 oz. glass of fluoridated tap or bottled water. Fluoridation of public drinking water began in 1939 when the Aluminum Company of America (ALCOA, the largest producer of aluminum in the world, and DOW,the largest chemical company in the world, decided to open manufacturing plants in Nazi Germany.

Many manufacturers made this move at the start of WWII in order to take advantage of the old Cabalistic expression, "War is business, and business is good!".

The Nazis began using fluoride in the water to sedate the general population and make them more docile and malleable to the control of Hitler's Third Reich. Back in America, the same multinational corporations had been poisoning and killing plants, crops, livestock, and people via the toxic fluoride-laden ash emitted from their smokestacks, while the US government manufactured and tested nuclear weapons by the dozens above ground.

Declassified files from the Atomic Energy Commission and the Manhattan Project now prove without a doubt that fluoridation of the water began as a way to negate the liability for fluoride contamination caused by above ground testing of nuclear weapons and the unregulated disposal of waste from aluminum smelters and similar manufacturing operations.

Knowing the public would soon be knocking down their doors demanding answers, the elite Cabal needed to come up with a way to blame the toxic side effects of their industries on something more benign and harder to detect.

This would not only help get rid of some of their unprofitable waste byproducts, but it would turn the public's attention elsewhere while the responsible parties slipped off into a dark corner to count their money. Having done this sort of thing many times before, the conspirators knew the general public would balk at the idea of putting chemicals in their water.

Early on, the American Dental Association (ADA) actually warned the public that "the potentialities for harm [in fluoridation] far outweigh those for the good." This little set-back led to the hiring of the master of subliminal mind control, Edwin L. Bernays, as the Illuminati public relations strategist. The nephew of Sigmund Freud, Bernays had an instant connection to the trusting public. In his book, Propaganda, Bernays explains how he used Freudian theory to manipulate the public using what he called "half-truths"

"A relatively small number of persons pull the wires which control the public mind," he boasted. Of course, Bernays knew full well the depth of his deception about fluoride and was proud of it.. His campaign to brainwash the masses into consuming poison for the benefit of the elite class was his primary claim to fame as the original "Doctor of Spin".

When even that effort didn't sufficiently sway the public, the satanic Illuminati turned to the classic bait and switch, appointing Oscar R. Ewing - a prominent lawyer for the Rockefeller-controlled ALCOA - as the head of the Federal Security Agency. This little maneuver all but assured the fluoridation of public water systems would go ahead as planned, no matter what the people wanted.

"Fluoridation is the greatest case of scientific fraud of this century, if not of all time," said Robert Carton, Ph.D. and former EPA scientist in 1992.

Fluoridation began as a way to camouflage and obfuscate responsibility for the contamination of water and earth by the industrial Illuminati war machine, but also as an intentional act to stunt and slow the brain development of future generations Hitler-style.

Today, the awake and conscious know fully well that fluoride calcifies and suffocates the pineal gland, a rice-sized organ located in the center of the brain just behind and above the pituitary gland. Modern humans didn't discover this gland until 1958, and even then they considered it to be a vestigial organ whose function ceased to exist during the course of our evolutionary history.

Yet, ancient peoples somehow innately understood this part of the human brain and believed it to have mystical powers. Often referred to as the third-eye (adopted as the all-seeing eye by the Illuminati), the pineal gland has long been considered to be the gateway between the physical and spiritual worlds. We still don't know everything there is to know about the brain, much less the pineal gland, but what we do know is vitally important.

We know that the pineal gland produces certain hormones including melatonin, which drives the human circadian rhythm. Melatonin's biggest role is in regulating the sleep-wake patterns that keep our brains and bodies healthy and energized. Melatonin is also believed to regulate female fertility cycles, and protect our hearts from cardiovascular disease and our bodies from cancer.

Fluoride is known to calcify the pineal gland and calcified plaque in the brain is known to be connected to various forms of dementia, including Alzheimer's disease.

From a spiritual perspective, damage to the pineal gland disrupts our connection to the Oneness of the universe and our connection to God. This ultimately brings about impaired perceptions of reality, which leads to confusion, depression, anxiety, and a whole host of other mental and neurological disorders.

The human body is approximately 75% water and the human brain, 85% water. All forms of fluoride are more easily absorbed by the body in an aqueous state. Fluoride also bio-accumulates in the body and crosses the blood-brain barrier, something that most substances and drugs do not do as a way to protect itself from foreign invaders.

One crucial aspect of the Illuminati's Agenda 21 is to poison the elixir of life. This not only destroys humanity's connection to the physical and spiritual worlds but also destroys their mental capacity to recognize the danger and sedates the drive needed to take control of the situation.

Ancient cultures had an instinctive awe and reverence for water equally as a life source and a divine force. Many have likened water to a living being, treating it - and all life on earth - with the respect given to gods and elders.

Today, we mostly just dump stuff in it and flush it away to who-cares-where. We run it through pipes for convenience and send it back into the world full of chemicals, drugs, and trash.

Then, after a quick run through the municipal sewage plant - which cannot and does not remove hormones, antidepressants, chemotherapy drugs and other autoimmune disruptors and carcinogens - it is treated to a healthy dose of brain and bone damaging chlorine and fluoride.

Once back in the main water supply, some money-hungry slickster simply takes it from the fluoridated municipal taps and bottles it in flimsy plastic bottles polished off with a fancy label that says "spring" something or other.

People pay good money for this "tasty and convenient" water, thinking that it's better to drink than tap water or corn-syrup-laden soft drinks. They keep it handy at all times and give it to their children to drink, even after it has sat in a hot car for days leaching plastic-based toxins like Bisphenol-A (BPA) into the biologically dead elixir and thus into our bodies.

Of course, we love our water. We like to play in it, touch it, look at it, and admire its beauty. Some even feel more connected to the whole when in the presence of pure wild water. Yet, the majority of modern culture no longer reveres water as a living, conscious being - giving it the respect and honor it deserves.

But that is about to change, for new research is confirming what ancient people have always known - water is alive.

And while they have tried hard to kill the living water, we've still got hope. Let's be clear about this - water is not alive because it moves or stirs our souls, it is alive because it has its own memory and consciousness. Modern research on water memory didn't really get going until Dr. Masaru Emoto, a Japanese researcher and author began working with vibrational energy, or what Emoto called "hado" in Japanese. In fact, Emoto described his work as "...the intrinsic vibratory pattern at the atomic level in all matter, the smallest unit of energy. Its basis is the energy of human consciousness".

Emoto had been energizing water by exposing it to different positive stimuli including, but not limited to healing spoken words and beautiful music. The vibrations of these sounds "energized" the water, which he then used to effectively heal people.

When his practice was brought into question, Emoto set out to prove that human consciousness directly influenced water's ability to heal.

He did this by taking photos of ice crystals made from the water he worked with. In his now-famous experiment, Emoto took regular water from a single source and divided it into two separate containers. One container had a positive word like "love" shown to it or spoken to it, while the other received a negative word like "hate". Drops of water from each container was then flash-frozen, observed and photographed.

The ice crystals that formed from the same exact water source but exposed to different words were remarkably unique from one another. The water exposed to a positive word had beautifully structured crystals, while those exposed to negative words were distorted, chaotic and sometimes even ugly.

He exposed water to all kinds of stimuli, from beautiful classical music to rock and roll, from words being spoken to it, to ignoring it all together. The results were consistent. Positive, peaceful, and beautiful thoughts, words, sounds, images, emotions, and other stimuli produced beautifully unique ice crystals, while their negative counterparts did not.

Since then, researchers around the world have replicated and confirmed Emoto's experiments and findings and taken them many steps further.

A laboratory in Israel recently used a similar protocol to Emoto's, but this time the water was dropped onto glass slides by different people. Each person made the same number of water drops on a glass slide. The drops were allowed to dry and then photographed using a dark-field microscope.

Each person's set of drops were exactly the same as one another, yet completely distinct from the other people's drops - much like fingerprints. Not unlike Emoto's ice crystals, each person's dried drops had unique circular structures.

The researchers applied the same technique in many more unique experiments, all of which pointed to the conclusion that water not only had memory but could quite literally connect, mirror and replicate anything it touched on a molecular level never seen before.

The revelationary documentary, Water Memory (2014), begins with the statement, "Water has the ability to reproduce the properties of any substance it once contained."

The study being discussed and shown in this epic work was begun by Nobel Prize Laureate, Professor Luc Montagnier. Despite being forced to do his research in a sub-par lab by his professorial co-workers who thought he was nuts, Montagnier continued to study the way water had the ability to hold, carry, and transmit very specific information to another and separate body of water.

After Montagnier's death, his friend and colleague Professor Guiseppe Vitiello picked up where Montagnier had left off.

Among other things, the two proved that water, having been purified of all matter, physically had the ability to create DNA strands merely by "listening" to a recording of water that had been inoculated with that exact DNA halfway around the world. A pure jar of water literally created an exact duplicate strand of DNA out of nothing but sound.

Our molecularly intimate physical and spiritual connection to water and sound are the driving force of all life on earth. If 75% percent of the human body is comprised of water and 85% percent of the brain is water, then water truly is the elixir of life.

And if water has the ability to remember, reflect, and reproduce both life and emotions like love, it also has the ability to do the same for hate and death.

This is something that the Cabalistic purveyors of dualistic spirituality and social Darwinian theories of intelligence and superiority have tried to do for thousands of years.

In a slow and insidious creep, this elite form of fascist eugenics is being used to fulfill the Illuminati's Agenda 21 for a New World Order reduction in the population. Their weapons of choice are not necessarily those of outright war, but more subtle tactics intended to divide, conquer and cull using any means necessary.

Fluoride, arsenic, aluminum, cadmium, lead and a whole host of neuro-damaging bisphynol and bisphynol A, which are found in plastic bottles, baby bottles, plastic food bags, food storage containers, and in the linings of canned foods. They are also found in chemicals used for dry cleaning, household cleaners, detergents and sanitizers, and in the plasticized inks on store receipts and in pretty much all commercial cosmetics, deodorants, and body products, including shampoos, deoderants, and lotions.

Once we consume these products, they and their toxic containers wind up in landfills, rivers, streams and oceans – like the Great Pacific Garbage Patch - where they continue to leach toxins into the elixir, killing the water and everything that relies on it for life – like us.

For many decades now, the powers that be have known about the toxicity of these and many other industrial chemicals. Yet, we the people, are just beginning to understand exactly how they affect the human brain and body. Those that affect the brain tend to mimic Alzheimer's and dementia, causing memory loss, brain fog, fatigue, insomnia, irritability, headaches, reduced fertility in men and women, and permanent damage on the cellular level. They disrupt our body's immune system from functioning correctly, resulting in autoimmune disorders, which have been rising to levels never seen before in human history. Still others cause cancer, organ failure, and general maladies like depression, chronic anxiety, insomnia, pain, inflammation and more. Most of the disease-like symptoms are actually forms of brain damage and cellular dysfunction at the DNA level.

The massive amount of toxins now found in our drinking water and in bodies of water that we rely on for food, drink, and even recreation are burning out the human brain and shutting it down like a light-dimming switch.

At the very least, these toxins weaken the brain and the immune system, which if healthy, would fight off true diseases naturally. But as it is the elixir of life is being destroyed with glutenous abandon. And by this act, the human population is not only being pacified and preoccupied with illnesses, but being slowly poisoned to death through the divine waters that we need in order to survive. But it doesn't have to be like that

Those who have had the cosmic fortune of having a true spiritual experience or revelation, fully understands that consciousness exists on many planes. If you believe in a Higher Power, then you also believe that everything is One and One is Nothing without Everything.

Indeed, researchers have begun to move from the idea of fission, which is the separation of principles to generate energy, to fusion, the bringing together of principles to generate energy. Only recently have researchers discovered that this simple understanding of reality will allow mankind to tap into a source of waste-free open-source energy that can free humanity from our current bondage to wasteful and polluting sources of energy and help us tap into less toxic ways to make and package products.

One of my she-roes, Vandana Shiva, speaks eloquently about violence and the homogenization of culture in Satish Kumar's deeply-moving book, You Are, Therefore, I Am. In it she says, "Rural people knew how to use the abundantly available nutrients of the forest plants, and the knowledge was handed down to them from generation to generation, but now that knowledge is fast disappearing under the influence of mono-crops and factory-made synthetic medicine. I call it monoculture of the mind."

This is such an appropriate and descriptive view of how we have allowed ourselves to become herded, misinformed, and myopic on the state of our natural world and how we, as a tribe of people, have put our faith in a single, violent, and myopic system that values money and power above all of the life on earth and the earth itself.

Isaac Newton eluded to that which modern man has forgotten when he said, "...what we don't know is an ocean."

As of yet, we don't know everything about the ocean and water in general, but we are re-learning what the Creator taught us in the beginning and that means respect for all of Creation. To change things for the better, we must increase the diversity of our information sources, open our hearts and minds, look beyond the corporate lies and have faith in the instinctive knowledge of ourselves and the beautiful garden we were given.

With this in mind, we must turn our attention to the holy water that is the true elixir of life. Think of what Emoto and others did when they turned loving energy towards water. We can do that on a grand scale.

There are other ways to use the memory of water to help heal water around the globe. It's called restructured water and the science of this is as fascinating as it is helpful. By introducing pure, clean, wild water to damaged, diseased, and dead water the structure of the dead water is restored to life. I know this may sound a bit hokey, but check it out. It's being done now with amazing results. But there is no time to lose. We must act now if we are to stop the Illuminati Agenda 21 elite from killing us with the thing we need the most. We can heal the God-given elixir of planet earth and all life can truly flourish once again.

CHAPTER 13

THE MEDICAL DEATH INDUSTRY

The United States of American is among the wealthiest nations on earth. We have what many believe is the best medical care available in the world, anywhere - but only to those who can afford it.

Yet, when compared to similarly wealthy and "developed" nations, America has a higher infant mortality rate, epidemic levels of obesity among adults and children, skyrocketing increases in mental illnesses and chronic diseases among young adults. There has also been an alarming rise in cases of Alzheimer's and other forms of dementia – not only in the elderly, but also in the young.

The increase in chronic diseases in children and young adults is particularly worrying to many health care givers. Type II diabetes, cancer, allergies, severe asthma, and autism spectrum disorder being of primary concern.

Many people were shocked, when in 2016 the US life expectancy actually began to drop. And you might be hard-pressed to find anyone you know that is not taking at least one pharmaceutical drug – a large portion of which are prescriptions for anxiety, sleeping disorders, depression, and pain. Opioid, heroin, and alcohol addiction have become epidemic - the former fueled by the Crown's Afghan opium monopoly.

Many of the causes of common chronic disease in America are obvious. Westerners typically eat more "pre-made", convenience, and processed foods and mixes low in nutrition, high in calories, corn syrup, added "nutrients", and unhealthy fats.

The US is renowned for food with unpronounceable additives, preservatives and fillers; laden with GMOs and Americans are probably the largest consumers of toxic sodas and energy drinks.

When it comes to food, many Americans - particularly the poor and working class - not only have fewer fresh food choices, but have been duped into the belief that convenience takes priority over a healthy diet.

Daily and abundant doses of fresh air, direct prolonged exposure to sunshine, and real physical exercise have been similarly discredited.

We've already talked about the poison elixir that the general public is forced to drink on a daily basis. In relation to the health-giving properties of living water, most tap water in the U.S. has horrible crystalline structure and is energetically dead.

We talked about dis-ease-causing heavy metals, industrial chemicals, and pharmaceutical drugs like fluoride, chemotherapy, hormones, and antibiotics - all of which are difficult to remove through typical water filtration.

Americans work longer hours with less time off than most other countries. This reduces sleep and taxes the adrenal glands, sending stress levels off the charts, which ultimately, shuts down our immune system - or, adversely, sends it into overdrive.

A cytokine storm is when the body overproduces immune cells and activating compounds known as cytokines. These chemical messengers send signals to the immune system. Sometimes it signals for a reduction in inflammation, but sometimes it does just the opposite. Diseases like lupus and the oft-misdiagnosed "Alzheimer's", among many other diseases, are awash in whirlwinds of unnatural cytokine storms.

Add to that the fact that living conditions for a vast majority of Americans is on the decline. Now referred to as the working poor, more and more Americans struggle with increasing levels of debt. Adjusted for inflation, we get paid less and have little savings compared to other wealthy nations. For most Americans, money doesn't go as far as it used to and everything costs more, leaving us living paycheck to paycheck and feeling powerless to change the system.

Because many American's financial situations are in the pits, they spend much less time vacationing and traveling, especially internationally. This small fact actually reduces our exposure to other culture's often healthier ways of living. Most other developed countries have more time off and personal time with family, have access to good public transportation, and much more market-fresh food choices.

Westerners, and now pretty much the rest of the world's population, watch too much TV, spend too much time on their phones, computers and video games and read fewer books, newspapers, and magazines than ever before.

For better or worse, we have been lured into the embrace of the Illuminati Surveillance and Mind Control Network, also known as the "technological revolution". The "Internet of Everything"Agenda 21 5G network will, in two years, expose everyone to the immune-killing and brain damaging effects of electromagnetic radiation emitted by billions of wireless and so-called "smart" devices connected to high-power, high-frequency, low-to-the-ground "small cell" radio frequency emitters every 100 yards or so.

This technology has led us like never before into a more sedentary lifestyle that keeps us indoors and away from natural sunlight and nature in general for the majority of our days.

The majority of people spend most of their waking hours completely bathed in the pineal-gland-killing light emitted from from fluorescent tubes, LED light bulbs, and electronic screens.

None of these artificial light sources are attuned to life as we know it. You can't grow plants in this light, so how can *we* expect to live in it - and be healthy.

The sun emits a measurable frequency of 528 Hertz of sound and 528 nanometers of light, which is the same frequency emitted by chlorophyll in plants and by the human brain. That's not a coincidence - that's Creation.

Life was Created in resonance with the wide spectrum of colors and sounds emitted by the sun, which is why ancient cultures often worshiped and revered it as a living being.

When we don't get enough real sunlight, we don't make our own vitamin D and our circadian rhythms are thrown out of whack, disturbing sleep/wake cycles, hormones, fertility, and the immune system as a whole - all of which are driven by the pineal gland in our brains.

When combined, these factors greatly reduce our body's ability to regenerate on a cellular level making us sluggish, chronically sick, and mentally deranged.

The Purveyors of Death were well-aware of the effects of artificial light when they decided to ban incandescent light bulbs, which actually had a half-way decent color spectrum that favored more relaxing reddish-orange hues over blue and white - light that is known to make humans prone to sleeping less and working more.

All of these alterable factors are enough to send any healthy immune system on a downward spiral leading directly to dis-ease in the body and mind, leaving the masses to degenerate slowly into a morass of devitalized energy, illness, and death.

And the sickest part is that those who push these products and agendas know it, full well. Yet, they don't do anything about it because it not only makes them rich and powerful, but ultimately, making people chronically ill is part of the Illuminati's long-range goal of eugenics and population control.

It only gets worse from here.

So many of those working in the traditional allopathic fields of health do not realize the harm that's been done to them and through them by official educators, politicians, government agencies, corporate drug pushers, and Illuminati liars of all stripes.

Much like the fluoride scam, there are countless ways to deceive and manipulate trusting people who believe so deeply in what they have been taught that they either do not even know that there are more effective and less toxic alternatives to treating disease than what the mainstream medical industry advocates. But they are all bought and paid for by so many medical-industry lobbies that it boggles the mind. It doesn't take a rocket scientist to see that the Illuminati Death Industry mantra now reads, "Illness is business and business is good... Really, really good."

The Big Pharma approach to healing the sick involves getting filthy rich while people suffer. Part of this is evidenced by laughably lax FDA regulations on pharmaceuticals with ridiculously biased, if any, peer-reviewed studies, a woeful lack of affordable generic drugs for common illnesses and infections, and multi-billion-dollar fear-based advertising campaigns aimed directly at consumers, which are not allowed in most other developed nations. Tack on huge industry perks and cash "incentives" from corporate drug pushers to medical practitioners, and lists of side effects that read like a horror novel.

Couple that with incredibly expensive health care available only to the wealthy. Those who can't afford it or are under-compensated by their insurance providers (or completely denied) are driven into life-long poverty. All the while the Medical Mafia "healthcare system" is being slowly consolidated and run by fewer and fewer "mega care providers" catering to the upper classes.

In 2018, the incidence of cancer and Alzheimer's is at epidemic levels, while the number of known and newly discovered viral diseases caused by ticks and mosquitoes occurring outside of their natural boundaries are on the rise. There was also a disturbing trend of relatively new autoimmune diseases cropping up in the general population, for which there are no known cures. Yet, the most disturbing and devastating medical apocalypse of our time has got to be the huge spike in autism, likely caused by an increase in required childhood vaccinations.

This hotly-debated topic, when carefully scrutinized, appears at the very least to be one of the largest cases of outright criminal fraud in the history of modern medicine and if not stopped right now, will be the impetus to convince the masses of the "value" of the Illuminati eugenics program in the near future.

The vaccination story starts innocently enough back in 1796 with Edward Jenner's smallpox vaccine. Eighty-nine years later, Louis Pasteur came up with the rabies vaccine. Relatively few people actually got these vaccines and when they did it was by choice, not by force.

It wasn't until the 1950's, when vaccines for diseases such as polio, measles, mumps, and rubella came onto the scene, that parents were forced to vaccinate their school-age children. At that time, they were given a total of five vaccinations. By the late 1960's, that number had risen to eight. Today, babies are automatically vaccinated against Hepatitis B at birth, even if they have no immediate risk for it. At two and four months, babies are given eight different vaccinations.

If parents follow the CDC's vaccination schedule, by the time a child is 6-years old they will have received 49 doses of 14 different vaccines. By the age of 18 (but often as early as age 9), children will have been given 69 doses of 16 vaccines! A ridiculous amount.

Nowadays, people between the ages of 19 and 65 are told by the CDC that they should also get yearly inoculations for influenza and multiple doses of Tdap (tetanus, diphtheria, pertussis), shingles (Zoster), Pneumococcal, Meningococcal, MMR (rubella), HPV (Human papillomavirus), Chickenpox (Varicella), hepatitis A and B, and Hib (Haemophilus influenzae), among others.

The vaccination cheerleaders bragging about all the new shots in the pipeline say, "Innovative techniques now drive vaccine research, with recombinant DNA technology and new delivery techniques leading scientists in new directions. Disease targets have expanded, and some vaccine research is beginning to focus on non-infectious conditions such as addiction and allergies."

While the government and medical establishment advocate the use of vaccinations, not everyone trusts the medical death machine to decide their efficacy or safety.

Many parents and doctors have witnessed first-hand the life-altering effects that vaccines have had on their children. Every vaccine is tainted with toxic adjuvants such as mercury, lead, iron, nickel, aluminum, arsenic, and chromium, not to mention the viruses themselves or the inactivated toxoid and biosynthetic bacteria used to make them.

In the 1960's, a polio vaccine produced by Merck was given to 200 children in Berkeley, California. Several of the children died immediately and many others were paralyzed for life.

When researchers began looking into the vaccine's safety, they found multiple cases of cancer among children that had received the vaccine during the previous ten years of use.

The deaths, paralyzations, and cancers were all caused by the Simian Virus 40 (SV40) strain of polio vaccine. They determined that the cause for all the deaths and illnesses stemmed from a virus found in the kidneys of the Rhesus monkeys that were used to make the vaccine.

In 1962, Dr. Bernice Eddy published her findings into the SV40 vaccine in a journal produced by the Federation of American Societies for Experimental Biology. Her findings revealed that "...an impressive list of oncogenic [cancer causing] viruses - the rabbit papilloma, polyoma, Rous sarcoma, the leukemia viruses . . ." were all found in SV40. The report clearly stated that the vaccine makers knew that these monkeys harbored such viruses, yet they continued to use the SV40 vaccine anyway.

A few years ago my oldest brother Patrick was diagnosed with glioblastoma brain cancer. During the course of research for alternative cancer therapies, we were shocked to find a study that revealed that adults, particularly men, who were given the SV40 polio vaccine as children in the 1960's were now developing glioma cancers at an alarming rate.

Merck knew back then that SV40 caused brain cancer. My brother died at the age of 54, a mere 18 months after being diagnosed. His brain cancer could very well have been caused by the polio vaccine he received as a child and the murderous bastards at Merck walked away scot-free yet again.

In 1987, an MMR vaccine made by Smith Kline Beecham was administered to children in Canada. Many soon came down with meningitis. The vaccine was quickly withdrawn, but instead of being destroyed as it should have been, it was sent to Britain and used on children with the same deadly results.

Once again the vaccine was withdrawn then sent to Brazil where it caused a massive meningitis outbreak. None of the pathological murderers at Smith Kline Beecham spent a single day in jail and they got to keep the billions of dollars they made maiming and killing innocent children.

Today, the entire world is faced with a biological apocalypse of such epic proportions that it makes the Bubonic Plague look like a day at the beach.

Autism was once a relatively obscure disease. The term "autism" was first used in the U.S. in 1940 to describe people who were withdrawn and socially removed, while the term Asperger's was being used for a similar condition in Germany.

Thousands of these injured adults were treated by the allopathic medical establishment using severe electroshock therapy and total isolation as the "cure".

In 1978, only 1 in 15,000 children was diagnosed with autism and even as recently as 2002, only 1 in 10,000 children were diagnosed with it. That number exploded to 1 out of 80 in 2014. The most recent statistics conclude that 1 out of every 45 children have some form of what is now called Autism Spectrum Disorder.

If the exploding trend in autistic children continues along this gradient, 1 in 3 children will be autistic by 2050. That means that within the next 32 years, one-third of the entire population will be mentally and/or physically disabled for life and will need full time care.

This horrific fact makes the Luciferian energy vampires incredibly happy because they feed off of pain and suffering. The autism crisis will leave families and the entire nation financially and emotionally shattered. People with autism can live a normally long life, but their needs will always be those of a sick child.

If this trend isn't stopped soon, the sheer number of people living with autism and the associated costs of caring for them will become a perfectly perverted opportunity for the introduction of the

Illuminati Agenda 21 eugenics program as a solution for the nation and the world.

The neurological nightmare called ASD is characterized by one or more behaviors including the lack of social interaction and communication with others, the inability to develop relationships, emotional or social withdrawal, the need to have repetitive daily patterns and routines, and physical abnormalities such as rocking, flapping, twirling, head-banging and the inability to sense emotions and events correctly.

Mounting evidence shows that the cause of the autism nightmare is mandatory childhood vaccinations. It now appears to all serious researchers that ASD occurs after toddlers receive their first MMR (measles, mumps, and rubella) combination vaccination at 12-15 months of age. This is the time when baby's brains are incredibly vulnerable and growing fast, as evidenced by their first words and first steps.

After receiving their MMR on schedule, parents are reporting symptoms such as rashes, fevers, convulsions, abnormally long and disturbing bouts of crying or screaming, head banging, loss of motor-coordination (walking, crawling), reduction or loss of speech (words, babbling), and loss of emotional response (smiling, eye contact, play). Many babies are reported to become listless and unresponsive - unable to hold a bottle or sit upright, and often exhibit many other disturbing behaviors not present prior to the vaccination.

What is apparent to almost everyone but the Merck-ants of Death and their Apologists is that autism is linked directly to the MMR combination vaccine.

The CDC recommendation for this vaccination is a two-dose series given at 12–15 months and again at 4–6 years. According their schedule, the second dose can even be given as early as four weeks after the first dose. This means that many children likely receive not only one dose at 12-15 months, but two doses only four weeks apart.

The cause is now known, but what people aren't talking about is the physical nature of the "dis-ease", which is for all intents and purposes a massive brain injury.

Like all the cases of vaccination injury that have come before, Merck and Friends know that its vaccination is causing injury to babies and will do nothing about it.

In fact, in a classic Luciferian move, Merck publicly denied that their combined MMR vaccine was causing any harm. And when it was suggested that perhaps the single dose vaccinations would not have the same outcome, Merck officials responded by withdrawing their individual single dose options from the market all together in order to protect their $30 billion dollar a year "MMR project".

As word got around, things got heated. Julie Gerberding, CDC Director from 2002-2009, was put in charge of investigating the rates of autism in relation to the MMR combo-vaccination on behalf of the people of the United States.

In the documentary, *Vaxxed: From Cover-Up to Catastrophe*, whistle-blower William W. Thompson, PhD, Senior Scientist for US Centers for Disease Control (CDC) said, "I was involved in deceiving millions of taxpayers regarding the potential negative side effects of vaccines. We lied about the scientific findings. The CDC can no longer be trusted to do vaccine safety work. They can't be trusted to be transparent. The CDC can't be trusted to police itself."

He said this because he was actually a part of the Illuminati cover-up to protect the wealth of Big Pharma - 50% of which is owned by the Rockefeller family. Thompson revealed that the CDC's own 2004 MMR vaccination study proved that children given the MMR vaccination on the CDC's schedule at 15 months old were more prone to developing autism.

The plot becomes more sinister when you take into account that the children who were most susceptible to this vaccine-induced brain damage were those that were perfectly normal and healthy during their first year of life. They were also predominantly male with African American boys being more than four times as likely to get autism than any other group.

This makes complete sense if you're a eugenics-loving Nazi psychopath, since black males are the most potentially revolutionary part of the population because of hundreds of years of institutional-scale racism and economic depravity.

Because of this, black men are notoriously difficult to brainwash, as has been proven by their tenacity and will to survive the City of London holocaust known as slavery, the violent backlash to the Civil Rights movement, and the modern day effort to dehumanize, criminalize, imprison and execute them in what amounts to 21st Century slavery.

If you want to control a population, it's important to take out the most rebellious males first. They are the ones who have the potential to physically overpower the scrawny Illuminati bankers and their ilk.

Of course, the FDA, HHS, and CDC all colluded to fudge the numbers to make the MMR study look rosy and sweet for the public so that parents would keep bringing their babies in for more shots and keep the money train rolling for their Babylonian handlers to the tune of 30 billion dollars a year for each vaccine on the market.

As for Julie Gerberding - she didn't spend a single day in jail for her murderous fraud, but rather knelt before her Luciferian bosses to receive her Merchant of Death Badge as she was promoted to President of Merck Vaccines in 2010.

She must have done something else equally as evil as the maiming and injuring of tens of thousands of little babies, because she was recently promoted again to the Executive Vice President and Chief Patient Officer, Strategic Communications, Global Public Policy, and Population Health at Merck & Co.

The Illuminati's Agenda 21 eugenics program includes plenty of mandatory vaccinations for the entire adult population and laws and new vaccines are in the works at this very moment.

Many healthy adults have been strong-armed with fear into accepting annual flu vaccinations and many employers now require it. The push is so strong that just about anyone can get a free flu vaccination at the local drug store even though they are immunologically strong enough to deal with the flu and can develop a stronger natural immunity to it if they do.

Is the flu vaccination the beginning of mandatory adult vaccination program and could it just possibly carry with it some Simian-like virus that causes cancer or cause the feminization of males and infertility of females in order to reduce the population?

Will vaccines be used to inject the population with microscopic bits of aluminum so the Chosen Ones can use EMFs from the ever-expanding cellular network to destroy our inert ability to harmonize with the natural frequencies of earth and make us more easy to track and control?

Do vaccinations cause severe mental fatigue and confusion to make it hard for us to find our will to rebel against fascist tyranny?

Will the next worldwide plague originate from mass vaccinations forced upon the people in order to prevent the next major social upheaval, which appears to be brewing at this very moment?

I don't know all the answers, but I certainly do not trust the Luciferian vampires that currently run the show. What I do know is that we must expose the Cabalists right now - stand in the brilliant light of the sun and connect with the energies of Creation.

Search out and use alternative health care practitioners and medical doctors that are versed in real alternative therapies to treat illness and disease.

Spend more time in the company of nature and those you love, rather than watching someone else's life unfold on Fakebook or other anti-social media. Go on vacation, get out of debt, and find a job you love - even if you won't make as much money.

Focus on eating clean nutritionally-dense food and drinking clean pure water that has been exposed to the sun, which resonates at the Creation Frequency of 528 Hz.

And last but not least, do not fear.

Good always conquers evil.

CHAPTER 14

CASTING THE WORLD WIDE INTER-NET

Imagine Darth Vader having Spider-Man's ability to cast a huge, inescapable web of evil over all of mankind in order to subvert, surveil, and subdue those who would oppose his reign and you have a full understanding of the World Wide Web and all the technology that goes with it. Indeed, just a few investigative queries show that every single one of our so-called technical advances were first developed and used by the military industrial complex as weapons of war.

The technology that 98% of the people on earth have been sold on for entertainment, socializing and to "make life easier", also happens to be the perfect tool for Orwellian-control of the masses and quite literally, a way to depopulate those deemed as "useless eaters". Everything you do or say on the internet is being recorded for posterity or for blackmail, whichever suits the Illuminati's needs. Mouth off, say too much, or get too close to the truth and you will quickly find out how "free" you really aren't.

Everyone likes to think they aren't addicted to their cell phones and other wireless tech but most are because the algorithms that run them were designed to be addictive. Aside from the social disorders that excessive cell phone use is causing across the board, there is one aspect to the "technological revolution" that the military, government, and the motley rich tech developers don't want you to know – the sound from your devices is killing you.

Maybe you remember the days of the dial-up modem where you sat for an eternity listening to screechy beeps and squeals as your phone connected your computer to the Worldwide Web or those that sometimes interfered with your radios, televisions, or telephones? Those sounds were generated as a result of electromagnetic radio frequencies (EMF) emitted from one device and picked up by the antennas on the others.

Humans can't normally hear the sound of electromagnetic energy pulsing through the air, but once you're able to hear it through EMF measuring instruments or device feedback, you really don't want to hear it again – and for good reason. Sounds like these, unlike natural sounds of rain or beautiful music, grate on the human ear like fingernails across a chalkboard and make people feel agitated, uncomfortable, and even angry because they are disharmonic and out of tune.

The effects of disharmonic frequencies on humans is a serious topic among product manufacturers, who understand that the sound their products produce has a direct effect on the "emotional quality" of the consumer, as explained in the abstract from proceedings at the 18th International Conference on Concurrent Engineering (ISPE), entitled, "Effect of Tonal Harmonic Feature in Product Noise on Emotional Quality".

Being comprised of mostly water, the human body is like a giant antenna that readily picks up electromagnetic frequencies in the environment. Our ability to tune into sound frequencies includes those that we can hear and those we cannot. Birds find their way south in the winter and north in the summer by tuning into the earth's natural magnetic frequencies.

Humans are like birds, bees, monarch butterflies and every other form of life on earth in that we were created to harmonize with the natural radio frequencies emitted by the earth and sun, which resonates at 528 Hertz of sound and 528 nanometers of light. Our brains emit 528 Hz of sound, as do green leaves and plants. It's not a coincidence or a manipulation of statistics - it's Creation.

Of course, we can't hear the sounds of the sun or of chlorophyll in plants. We can't hear the stars and other planets with our ears. But that doesn't mean we don't feel and hear them with our body and mind. In fact, NASA and other astral observers have been recording the sounds of space for a long time. Every planetary body in our solar system resonates with beautiful harmonic frequencies – all but earth, that is.

Earth most assuredly sounded that way at one time but these days, our beautiful blue planet sounds like demonic metal grinding over death. It is not pleasant to listen to, yet that is exactly what our bodies "hear" with our internal antennas every day of our lives. This is caused by all the electromagnetic sound smog, which now covers our planet like a thick veil that is not only drowning out the earth's natural harmonic sound as heard from space, but is also changing the pulse, or heartbeat, of Earth itself. If we humans were created to function perfectly in the presence of harmonic frequencies, then it makes sense that discordant frequencies made by unnatural sources have a negative impact on our emotions and biological functions.

Just as our government and military industrial complex have known about harmonic frequencies and their correlation to life on earth, they also know that sound can be used as a weapon that kills. One example of a modern sound weapon is the LRAD (Long Range Acoustic Device) Sound Cannon, which causes extreme pain to anyone within 100 meters of its 30 degree-wide aim. The military-grade version of this weapon can transmit voice commands and debilitate listeners up to five and a half miles away, causing permanent hearing loss and the inability to move. Other examples come from the Department of Defense Advanced Research Projects Agency (DARPA) and friends. These weapons come in many forms, including directed-energy weapons (DEW) that use highly focused energy waves emitted as lasers, microwaves, and particle beams.. There's Pulsed Energy Projectiles (PEP), which emit an infrared laser pulse that shoots expanding plasma and stuns, paralyzes, and causes extreme pain and the Electrolaser, which sends electric currents down an ionized plasma track to immobilize, stun or kill victims.

Probably one of the biggest and nastiest of the known energy weapons comes from your friends at the High Frequency Active Auroral Research Program, which goes by the angelic acronym, HAARP - yet another super-high-power, high-frequency radio transmitter brought to you by DARPA. The publicly-claimed purpose of HAARP is "...to conduct pioneering experiments in ionospheric phenomena" and assess its ability to be used for developing "enhancement technology for communications and surveillance".

Yet, the military-grade weapons our government (and others) use regularly aren't nearly as insidious as those that we have been slowly conditioned to both want and need. We embraced them wholeheartedly and welcomed them into our homes and lives believing they were not only safe but would make our lives "better". Yet, emerging research indicates that since the introduction of cell phones and the internet into the public sphere, the shit has really hit the fan. For the last 20 years, HAARP has been working hard on manipulating and weaponizing the weather. They call it "geoengineering", but it goes much, much further than that.

If you weren't sure before, make no mistake now - chemtrails are real. In fact, in mid-2018, President Donald Trump actually made a public statement saying that he wanted chemtrail spraying to end.

Chemtrails are aerosolized chemicals laden with nano-particles of aluminum, strontium, barium, fluoride and a number of other toxins that are "seeded" into our lower atmosphere. Eventually, these particles drift to earth and are ingested and inhaled by everything that breathes and absorbed by the roots of plants, trees, and food crops. The levels of aluminum that have been found in water, food, and all biological life forms in the last 10 years are simply staggering.

Dig into this terrifying rabbit hole and you will find Morgellon's(Google that one if you want to be really freaked out), explosive wildfires, dying forests, the disappearance of insect and bird life, starving salmon, whales grounding themselves on shore, bleaching coral reefs and a whole host of other creepy life-sucking dis-eases.These nano-metals are now inside of nearly every living organism and when exposed to the extremely high EMFs from HAARP, cell towers and wireless devices, our bodies become living antennas and lead to radiation damage on a cellular level.

Electromagnetic frequencies (EMFs) emitted from all forms of wireless technology – wireless keyboards, laptops, cell phones, iPads, tablets, FitBits, gaming devices, smart meters, smart everything, and much more - are now *the* most prevalent disharmonic frequency on the face of the earth (and probably in space, as well).

More than a decade ago, California health officials warned that "long-term use of cell phones—which emit electromagnetic radiation when they send and receive signals from towers or WiFi devices—can affect human health.".

They also stated that, "...some laboratory experiments and human health studies have suggested the possibility that long-term, high use of cell phones may be linked to certain types of cancer and other health effects" including brain cancer, tumors of the acoustic nerve and salivary glands, lower sperm count, headaches, and effects on learning, memory, hearing, behavior and sleep. But it wasn't until 2017 that a member of UC Berkeley's School of Public Health sued the state in order to have the study released to the public.

This is but one study among thousands that link wireless technology with widespread, life-threatening human and animal diseases and cellular malfunctions that include cancerous tumors, blood abnormalities, reduced sperm and egg counts, hearing loss, ringing in the ears, headaches, and decreased well-being, among others.

As far back as 1998, Polish researchers found that non-ionizing radio frequencies promote cellular mutations that lead to cancer and leaks between the blood-brain barrier caused by changing the calcium ion activity in cells, which in turn regulates central and peripheral nervous system health, membrane integrity and energy production. In a nutshell, wireless technology is the vaccine, fluoride, tobacco, lead paint, and mercury filling scandals all rolled into one massive low-frequency armpit of Luciferian stench.

Many people are still skeptical of the warnings about the dangers of EMF's because they really don't want to give up the convenience of their cell phones and the fun of their other wireless devices. But the truth is out there for anyone to see.

A working group of scientists from 14 countries meeting at the World Health Organization's Agency for Research on Cancer (WHO/IARC) looked at dozens of peer-reviewed studies on the effects of EMF's from cell phones and wireless devices. They determined that cell phones were "possibly carcinogenic" and listed them as 2B carcinogens - a category that includes toxic chemicals and pesticides like fuel exhaust, dry cleaning chemicals, and the banned pesticide DDT. "A review of the human evidence of epidemiological studies shows an increased risk of glioma and malignant types of brain cancer in association with wireless-phone use," said Dr. Jonathan Samet, the chairperson of the IARC working group. If you aren't sure, glioblastoma is a death sentence.

Research has long shown electromagnetic radiation to be harmful to the human body. The primary factors involved in physiological harm correlates directly to the frequency of the radio waves, the strength of transmission, and the duration of exposure. A comparison of the radio frequencies used over the last few decades with those of the new 5G (and future YG) wireless networks reveal a massive increase in frequency levels and types of radio waves being employed.

Cell phones became a popular and affordable item in the late 90's. Before that, they were big, bulky and expensive. Phones operating in the 2G and 3G networks operated at 800 and 1900 (1.9) MHz respectively. With the demand for faster service, the 4th Generation Wireless (4G) utilized frequency realms of from 700 MHz at the very lowest and cheapest range, to the more common 2500 (2.5) MHz range. The latter just happens to be the same exact frequency at which water molecules begin to oscillate (spin). Until then, these super-high frequencies were only used by commercial

airlines and the military for radar, sonar, and communications -
and, of course, for frequency weapons, torture, and brainwashing.

The new 5G, which is currently being installed and tested in
several major metropolitan areas and scheduled to be fully
operational nationwide by 2020, is going to operate at a death-
inviting minimum of 6000 (60.0) GHz (that's giga-hertz!), which is
basically 1,000,000,000 (one-billion) Hertz! This is literally mind-
blowing because it is at this frequency that the body binds and
absorbs oxygen. Seriously?

In other words, the Illuminati 5G network will not only starve
humans of their ability to uptake water and oxygen, the two most
essential elements to our lives, our health, and our natural
resonance with the earth and Creation, but it has been proven
through the US military's own studies and documentation to have
the ability to mutate and destroy the molecular structure of every
part of the human and animal body. If I were to condense all this
information to make it short and sweet and to the point so that no
one misunderstands the situation: EMFs from 5G can permanently
alter your DNA and kill you.

Now, if that weren't enough, it is very popular to have a cordless
walk-around home phone as a landline. These conveniences first
came to market in the '80's and operated on a radio band frequency
of around 1.7 to 50 MHz. The 90's models operated at roughly 900
Hz. Today's DECT or Digital European Cordless Telephones
operate between 1.9 - 5.9 GHz, but most use the higher band
frequency. This makes these ubiquitous devices even more
powerful than cellular phones using the current 4G network. Many
experts are suggesting that modern cordless DECT phones are even
more dangerous than cell phones - emitting as much EMF's as a cell
tower near your home. Both the phone and the deck of these units
emit the same mind-blowing levels of EMF's, which is essentially
microwave radiation.

The new and astounding speeds of 5G are brought to you, not by
the current form of radio waves being used, but by shorter and
more powerful millimeter waves. These waves have not been used
in this way before because they don't travel long distances or

penetrate physical obstacles like walls and trees very well. Because of this, 5G can only operate well if the transmitters (cell towers) and receivers (devices) are very close together.

To achieve this closer distance requirement, cell tower antenna arrays must be much closer to the ground and connected by a daisy-chain of "small cell" transmitters placed roughly 100-200 yards apart to efficiently move the frequency around objects that it cannot pass through. Look around you and pay attention to the cell towers in your area. Not only are they erecting new towers closer and closer together, but they are dropping the arrays closer and closer to the ground.

I've actually seen cell towers with arrays that have been re-positioned so that they are just above the treetops and typically within 30 feet of rooftops. In order to connect the world to the Internet of Things, hundreds of thousands of new cell towers are being erected and located only hundreds of yards from of each other. These larger, lower cell towers will soon be connected to literally billions of "small cell" transmitters at ground level in order to further extend the reach of the short millimeter waves around obstructions like trees and buildings.

These mini-cell-towers are very innocuous. Most are less than 3 feet tall and are being mounted to stop lights, street lights, electric poles, lampposts, and flagpoles, as well as being attached to the lower floors of homes and buildings and overpasses. Many are being dressed up to look like just another part of the architecture or disguised as trees or cacti or other "natural" features to make them hard to spot. Soon, there will be small cell emitters every 200 yards or less. By 2019, you will most likely have one or more of these new high-energy weapon systems in your front or backyard or on the roof or facade of your home, workplace, or school where their super-high radio frequencies can bombard you and your children's brains day in and day out.

The total assault on humanity began in 1992 with the Trojan Horse known as UN Agenda 21. We have endured so much already: the introduction of the internet and wireless communications to homes, schools, and workplaces around the globe; the forcing of

GMOs and their associated pesticides into the global food system; an unprecedented uptick in the frequency of childhood and adult vaccinations; an increase in weather modification and chemtrail activity from our friends over at HAARP; the introduction of the CERN psychopaths who happily collide the "God Particle" for shits and giggles; and the advent of a permanent war economy.

It's time for people to wake up to the fact that humans are soon to join the endangered species list and that the Illuminati hunters do not have your interests in mind and are not just out sight-seeing.

Tom Wheeler, who was the Obama Administration's FCC Chairman and a long-time tool of the telecommunications cartel. Under his guidance, he almost assured the telecom and tech industry free reign when he gave a long and very disturbing speech about how no regulations will be enacted to curtail the new "Internet of Things". He said, "Unlike some countries, we do not believe we should spend the next couple of years studying what 5G should be, how it should operate... Turning innovators loose is far preferable to expecting committees and regulators to define the future. We won't wait for the standards to be first developed... Instead, we will make ample spectrum available and then rely on a private sector-led process for producing technical standards best suited for those frequencies and use cases."

So, next up for planet earth and its inhabitants is the miraculous 5G Network, which will take our current exposure to radio frequency radiation into the stratosphere and allow the maniacal corporations of the Crown to "Ensure" that everything you own has super-enhanced Artificial Intelligence that is way "smarter" than you are – and better looking and funnier, too.

And while you're dying of EMF cancer or some other exotic disease no one has ever heard of before, your personal droid will lock you out of your own home to live with the other biologicals in the wild - leaving them, their Illuminati Masters, and a few mind-altered human slaves to tend to their privatized Garden of Eden. God help us all.

CHAPTER 15

2016 ILLUMINATI ELECTION NIGHTMARE

The June 2016 premature crowning of Hillary Clinton as the US Democratic nominee for president by the Rothschild-controlled AP was key to suppressing voter turnout in the crucial California primary. This combined with the massive voter disenfranchisement in the Golden State sealed the fate of the latest and possibly last attempt at political revolution in America, as embodied by the Bernie Sanders campaign.

The Rothschild-led Illuminati lizard bloodline banksters depend on a climate of fear and negativity to maintain and increase their control over the global populace. Remember, the Masonic project is about turning us into batteries to generate negative energy for their 4th dimension nightmare.

The general election match between Druid Council war witch Hillary Clinton and Rothschild mob strawman Donald Trump created a perfect negative energy nightmare scenario for the US.

Trump duped many good people into believing he was a maverick, though in fact he is a Rothschild tool and Crown Agent. He was used as a strawman when he bought long-time CIA drug money laundry Resorts International in 1987, along with a bunch of ocean-front property that would be turned into the Atlantic City boardwalk. The Illuminati got its East Coast dirty money gambling site, while Trump was bailed out of bankruptcy by Rothschild Inc. bond specialist Wilbur Ross, who was rewarded with his post as Commerce Secretary. Trump was rewarded with the Presidency.

This Crown Agent vs. Crown Agent match-up created a climate of fear, hopelessness, anger, and division that the Illuminati then used to temporarily derail the Truth Movement so they could push forward with their final solution trans-humanist 5G agenda.

The hatred and vitriol coming from both sides towards the other reached dangerous levels, further feeding the blood lust of the Anunnaki lizards and their cousin Luciferians who run this planet as their slave plantation.

Their infrastructure, now built out by us slaves, jobs will become more scarce and the Crown will use this bad energy vortex to push forward with their desired 75% depopulation of the planet.

This climate of negativity, combined with the ongoing mass addiction to all things Internet, has stripped many of their humanity already. Elon Musk and other tech gurus now openly talk about how their quantum computers are summoning demons. But the demons are already here.

The rise in US school shootings, for example, can be directly correlated with the coming of the Internet. Chaos is the Luciferian goal and will cause human culture to degenerate. They will then use this chaos to justify a micro-chipped population, a digital crypo-currency and 5G enslavement.

Cataclysmic events such as WWIII, a massive stock market crash and ensuing depression, or a sudden reversal of the North Atlantic current could all be used to usher in this final solution New World Secular Order.

Order out of Chaos - the self-proclaimed modus operandi of the Freemasons - will be deployed more frequently, as fear overtakes the rational mind of the public.

In a worst-case scenario, we could see an outright alien invasion of this planet, as the Dark Star Planet X Nibiru - home to the Anunnaki - looms ever closer. Scientists at CERN who are arrogantly attempting to identify the "God particle" have begun to see demons. Luciferian brain worship, reinforced by the internet, acts as a homing beacon, calling the Anunnaki back to planet Earth

During the coming months it will become difficult for people to simply stay human. I recommend disengaging from the political party two-camp illusion as soon as possible.

Disengage too from Facebook and all Internet communication. The aliens are using it to ostracize rebels and create a hive consensus that reinforces negativity. Social media is anti-social. Depend instead on nature and real human interaction to guide your thoughts and feelings.

The epic battle is upon us. Put simply - because it is simple - it will be a contest between good and evil, between nature and technology, between God and Satan, between high-frequency humans and low-frequency 4th dimension lizard-brain aliens. Make sure you pick the right side. You won't get a second chance.

CHAPTER 16

INTERNET PSYOPS
AND THE COMING COLLAPSE

Due to the fear-based political polarization that the well-orchestrated Trump/Clinton presidential match up produced, the wheels of this once-great nation appear to be coming off.

There was the Orlando false flag prosecuted by a Wackenhut agent, countless white supremacist police assassinations of black people and the Dallas response to that, a supposedly populist Brexit that was actually engineered by the City of London banksters and, quite appropriately and not coincidentally, a record heat wave throughout the nation.

Rothschild lieutenant George Soros has sold his US stock portfolio in favor of a short position on the US stock market, saying that in a best case scenario we are in for a deflationary depression, while at worst there will be riots and a class war in America. He ought to know, since his Crown handlers are fomenting it.

Deutsche Bank - the Nazi-funding Warburg family wealth repository that made a killing shorting the airline and insurance stocks negatively affected by 911 - is reportedly sitting on $40 trillion in bad derivative bets and is offering a ludicrously high 5%

CD to the public to illustrate its desperation. The Federal Reserve has marked their US division as "troubled".

The stock buyback machine that has been propping up stock markets around the world is running out of gas. People still aren't buying anything. Factories are operating at record-low production levels. Personal debt is piling up again. And more youth are living in their parents' basements, trying to dodge the student loan police.

Another housing market bubble is in its late stages, as the same big banks who caused the 2008 housing crash, then swallowed up those foreclosed houses on courthouse steps across the US, are now offering the same no-money-down loans to poor people now looking to buy houses as they did in the decade that preceded the crash.

Amidst this cultural and economic carnage, an increasing number of Americans are addicted to the internet and all things electronic. They are increasingly urbanized and landless and much less self-reliant than their parents' and especially their grandparents' generation. Most people, like America, produce absolutely nothing.

Instead, they spend their lives hardwired *en masse* into matrix machines and taken "on-line" in much the same way a nuclear reactor is brought online to produce negative, combative and disagreeable energy, this time in chat rooms, Facebook groups and similar social engineering hive-mentality projects of the global elite. This negativity is rocket fuel for the global elite, be they inbred Rothschilds, aliens, the Devil or simply heartless machines.

They are, in fact, all of the above.

And you are being used as their on-line batteries. You are, as the late great former American Indian Movement (AIM) counter-intelligence chief and poet/musician John Trudell stated, "being mined".

You are being deprived of oxygen and water and transformed into metal, so that you can be mined.

Kindness, decency and integrity have become "uncool". Spiritual grounding has given way to phony electronic-based fashion shows of all sorts, with the posers trying in very great vain to be the smartest person in the room, all the while getting dumber.

Everyone seems to talk in the same dispassionate monotone voices, whether their position is open white supremacy (Trump) or scared political correctness that doesn't much mind corruption and cheating (Clinton). People are starting to sound like robots.

The Internet - founded by the Pentagon's DARPA under the guise of "liberating the information flow for a more democratic world" - is in fact creating a world of character-devoid mono-culture machines who think and talk the same and have only a vague and fleeting resemblance to their former humanity.

Petitions are signed, virtual groups are formed, debates are engaged in, yet if the lumpen mass of on-line negative-energy drones were to look out their air-conditioned windows - and most won't - they would actually see that living conditions continue to deteriorate rapidly, the planet gets increasingly trashed, families are being torn apart by the selfishness and narcissism produced by machine addiction and survival skills do not exist.

Life-experience has been tossed over the side in favor of whatever Wikipedia or Ask Jeeves says about it. Everyone knows everything about…well…everything. People talk too much. No one listens. The information overload produces indecision, isolation, insecurity fragmentation and confusion in people.

The old ways of the ancients are discredited as "Luddite", when in fact these are the ways that will save us from this beast.

All the while the "expert drones" who have positioned themselves as Internet gatekeepers get dumber, more detached from reality, and frighteningly amoral.

The most recent example of this was a black woman in Minneapolis whose boyfriend had been shot by a white supremacist cop during a routine traffic stop. It was creepy enough to watch the cop screaming like the demented psychopath that he is on the video from the women's all-important "smart" phone.

Far more disturbing was the fact that the woman was so busy narcissistically filming the situation for her Fakebook friends and sycophants that she neglected to help her dying boyfriend in any way. He died, but hey, she's famous. Isn't that what really matters?

In the coming months there will be a financial collapse that will make the 1930's look like a walk in the park. The biggest banks will fail due to the aforementioned derivatives, taking down most other smaller banks, the stock markets, commodities (including gold), housing and all else with it.

Without a functioning banking system, grocery shelves could go bare, the lights may well go out, hopefully the Internet will go down, the fake election will become irrelevant and World War III - given the current and very dicey geopolitical situation - could easily be started by an unhappy electronic accident.

Preppers who have tried to buy their way to survival will perish along with the others beside their gasless generators, rotting freezer food, and empty computer screens. The "expert" Internet drones will be helpless, city dwellers will go even more crazy than they already have and millions could well die in the riots and starvation that ensue.

The elite's drone weaponry - now well-tested on the fake ISIS and in Gaza - will be turned on unruly citizens, all easily located using their tracking device cell phones. Never more exposed due to the "Web", people's bank accounts, mutual funds and life insurance policies will be looted by bankers disguised as hackers who are waiting in the wings for just this event.

It will suddenly dawn on many that the Internet really was a City of London drag net and that they have been had. At this point the only thing that will matter is a survival skill set and cooperation - two very human matters that are threatened with antiquity by the machines.

CHAPTER 17

SMART PHONES MAKE DUMB PEOPLE

This morning our yard was abuzz with a chorus of songbirds. summer tanagers, vireos, orioles, indigo buntings, goldfinches and cardinals that had joined the resident bluebirds, woodpeckers, Virginia creepers, nuthatches, titmice and sapsuckers to complete the ensemble.

Many had come in flocks, which was unusual before a few years ago. We live in a remote area, far from any cell phone towers. As these towers have become more ubiquitous the flocks of birds coming here have increased. Others in urban areas say their songbirds have disappeared altogether. Many urban people are also reporting a massive decline in insect populations.

With the discovery of the Schumann resonances in 1952, it became apparent even to mainstream scientists that the earth was an electromagnetic living organism that constantly emits extremely low-frequency (ELF) waves.

Birds and insects use these frequencies as a compass when migrating. Many studies have demonstrated the adverse effects that the spike in artificial ELF waves have had on birds and insects. Colony collapse in honey bees has been connected to these same

ELFs. Hundreds of species of birds and butterflies will soon be extinct. These are the canaries in the coal mine for a coming mass extinction event.

Human health is also being severely damaged by this explosion in radio waves.

The earth's electromagnetic field surrounds and protects us, operating at an average natural frequency of 7.83 Hertz. Solar winds, lightning and other natural phenomenon act to maintain this average by adding or subtracting energy when necessary. This is the heartbeat of Mother Earth.

Since humans are of this earth, we are electromagnetic beings. Just look at an EKG (electrocardiogram) screen in any hospital and this becomes obvious. In the 1980's it was discovered that the human brain also has an operating frequency - the exact same as the Schumann resonance at 7.83 Hertz.

Austrian electrical engineer Lewis Hainsworth discovered these naturally occurring brain frequencies, which have become known as alpha waves. Hainsworth was the first to suggest that human health is dependent upon our brain frequency being in sync with the earth's Schumann resonance.

One of the main researchers on the topic, Dr. Wolfgang Ludwig, discovered that while the Schumann resonance could be easily measured in nature and out at sea, it was nearly impossible to detect in cities or even smaller towns where cell phone towers and usage are omnipresent.

More ominously Hainsworth predicted that should humans continue to be exposed to these unnatural frequencies, an evolution of the human brain was likely. But an evolution into what?

We would be evolving from a hundred thousand year state where we were happily tuned into Mother Earth's natural rhythms, to a state of chaos and discontent based on an unnatural and therefore Alien/AI life cadence.

Does this explain the multiple personality, identity scrambling trans-gender, trans-humanist push by the Illuminati's Tavistock Institute media branch? Does it explain why people seem to be going completely nuts? What happens when 5G gets completely rolled out? Will humans be in the same boat as birds? Will we completely lose our bearings as to who we are and be herded that much more easily into New World Secular Order City of London-orchestrated depopulation and disease?

Despite the lack of both telecom regulation and funding for studies critical of ELFs, even mainstream organizations like to WHO now admit that cell phones cause cancer, the most common form of which are gliomas located in the area of the brain nearest the ear. Many of these gliomas then migrate to the pineal gland at the center of the brain. This is significant for two reasons.

Physiologically, the pineal gland is where we produce melatonin. This human hormone attacks free radicals and is key to rebuilding our badly taxed immune systems, which most researchers agree is the main culprit behind not just cancer but all disease.

We produce melatonin only when we sleep in a dark place, due to our innate circadian rhythm. But recent studies have shown that our brain cannot distinguish between light frequency and ELFs. So if you live in an area congested with cell phone chatter, you are not producing melatonin because your brain doesn't think you're asleep even when you are.

Spiritually, the pineal gland was regarded by the ancients as our "third eye", giving humans a natural ability to detect phenomenon existing beyond our five-senses. Many Illuminati researchers have documented the obsession these self-professed Luciferians have had with shutting down this God-given ability based in our pineal gland in the entire human population, and hoarding this knowledge for themselves via their secret societies.

If we are to remain human, we must expose this well-marketed onslaught of radio waves for what it is: an assault on both humanity and our earth Mother by an alien/AI invader.

Get off your "device", get outside and get to know both your Mother and yourself. Then fight like hell to defend both of you, because this is a war they have declared on all of us. Now if you'll excuse me, I have some birds I need to get in tune with.

CHAPTER 18

CAMBRIDGE ANALYTICA
FACEBOOK MI6 PSYOP

If ever there was smoking gun evidence as to who is behind the constant manipulation of global geopolitics, it is the 2018 scandal involving Facebook and Cambridge Analytica. The case unravels the Gordian knot that binds British and Israeli intelligence in the service of the City of London Crown bankers.

I have long contended that Mark Zuckerberg's Facebook is an Israeli Mossad intelligence operation designed to gather a dossier on every person on the planet, while destroying the social fabric necessary to challenge banker hegemony via disinformation, division and conflict creation, and also damaging the emotional well-being of humanity through cleverly orchestrated psychological warfare.

Cambridge Analytica is a British "data mining" firm, whose logo is a brain with vectors connecting dots. It was spun off from its parent firm SCL (Strategic Communications Laboratories) Group in 2013 to "participate in American politics".

Cambridge and Oxford Universities in the UK are incubators for the global banking elite, producing - as do Harvard and Yale in the US - the managerial class for the Rothschild Illuminati.

Cambridge Analytica insider Robert Mercer was an early pioneer in artificial intelligence and is a major funder of far-right US groups like Heritage Foundation, Cato Institute, Breitbart.com and Club for Growth. He resides at "Owl's Nest" mansion in New York.

Mercer was also the biggest funder of Brexit, via Nigel Farrage and the UK Independence Party. While many see Brexit as emancipation from EU tyranny, I have long contended that it was orchestrated by the elite to cement the Anglo-American alliance and to insulate the City of London banks from incoming EU regulations on their dirty activities.

Mercer himself was named as a director of eight different Crown-controlled Bermuda-based firms implicated in tax evasion by the leaked Paradise Papers.

But a recent British Channel 4 undercover investigation has revealed far more nefarious activities that make Cambridge Analytica and Facebook look an awful lot like a well-orchestrated British/Israeli intelligence operation. In fact it is a textbook example of how the now silent British Empire still runs the world using its Israeli and US surrogates.

About twelve minutes into the interview Cambridge CEO Alexander Nix is caught on camera bragging about how British companies often "subcontract" work to Israeli firms since they are, "very effective in intelligence gathering".

The undercover reporter for Channel 4 News posed as an operative for a wealthy client hoping to get certain candidates elected in Sri Lanka.

Nix told the reporter, "...we're used to operating through different vehicles, in the shadows, and I look forward to building a very long-term and secretive relationship with you."

Nix then brags about how Cambridge and its parent SCL Group have secretly manipulated elections in over 200 countries around the world, including Nigeria, Kenya, Czech Republic, Argentina and India.

Cambridge used bribes, prostitutes and fake IDs to engineer election outcomes. Nix describes the honey traps his firm set to discredit certain candidates where they would, "send some girls around to the candidate's house. Ukrainian girls are very beautiful. I find that works very well."

It is no coincidence that one of the biggest MI6/Mossad operations in recent years was the Ukrainian coup that brought billionaire Petro Poroshenko and his Zionist mafia to power. White slavery is a trademark of British intelligence, where pedophilia is rampant.

The spin-off of Cambridge in 2013 now gave the Illuminati direct access to manipulate the 2016 US presidential election. While the City of London pushes the fake Russiagate narrative, it now appears it was the City of London that engineered the Trump victory in an attempt to further nullify the American Revolution.

They did it using an Israeli "subcontractor" called Facebook, which fed data to Cambridge while GCHQ was busy monitoring the Trump campaign to make sure their soon-to-be-played "trump card" was going to do as he was told.

But Cambridge wasn't just mining the data from Facebook. Recently uncovered memos reveal that it was manipulating the data with Facebook's knowledge to "create desired emotional states" in users. In other words it was an MK-ULTRA type mind control operation on a massive scale.

As Nix brags in the interview, "We just put information into the bloodstream of the internet, and then watch it grow, give it a little push every now and again... like a remote control. It has to happen without anyone thinking, 'that's propaganda', because the moment you think 'that's propaganda', the next question is, 'who's put that out?'. Many of our clients don't want to be seen to be working with a foreign company... so often we set up, if we are working then we can set up fake IDs and websites, we can be students doing research projects attached to a university, we can be tourists, there's so many options we can look at. I have lots of experience in this."

There it is. Straight from the Crown Agent "subcontractor's" mouth. Naturally, on May 18, 2018 Cambridge Analytica declared bankruptcy, a move that will seal its records in a court of British Maritime law for a good long while. Thank goodness the inbred lizards can still count on Oxford Analytica.

God Hang The Queen!

CHAPTER 19

TECH ADDICTION & THE ILLUMINATI AGENDA

In a 2018 open letter the two largest investors in Apple - Jana Partners and The California State Teacher's Retirement System - called on the tech giant to take a serious look at how increased screen time is affecting and addicting children to technology.

The letter said, "Apple can play a defining role in signaling to the industry that paying special attention to the health and development of the next generation is both good business and the right thing to do."

While a handful of commentators have railed against the dangers of a world operating in "augmented reality" mode, could this letter be a bellwether towards a quantum leap in societal awareness as to the dangers of technological addiction on a mass scale? Let's hope so.

With CERN opening Pandora's box in its arrogant quest for the "god particle", increasingly powerful cell phone towers are said to be broadcasting CERN-generated dark matter into American households.

Additionally, demonic "pay with your face" portals are now in the hands of nearly every American - child and adult alike. We are at a spiritual crossroads on planet earth.

Illuminati programming on both TV and the Internet is coming out in the open. The latest Taco Bell commercials contain a tacit and triumphant admission of the secret societies' existence.

On November 13 the FDA approved the first-ever micro-chipped prescription drug. Abilify MyCite contains a "digital ingestion tracking system" that will record whether or not the patient took his/her medication.

And now corporate retailers like Walmart and Tommy Hilfiger are embedding invisible RFID tags and microchips in the clothing and other "goods" you buy, which allow them to literally track your every move, how often you wear or use the item, and much more personal data. The Illuminati end game is nigh. And technology is their spearhead.

Ironically, it is disCERNment that now becomes paramount, as the Tavistock media step up their deception and perception management as to who are the angels and who are the demons. Social media is their favorite venue.

In November 2017 former Facebook president Sean Parker himself stated of the social media platform, "God only knows what it's doing to our children's brains."

Another top former Facebook executive Chamath Palihapitiya stated the obvious solution, "I can control my decision, which is that I don't use that shit. I can control my kids' decisions, which is that they're not allowed to use that shit."

Those who choose to remain addicted to their cell phones, tablets and laptops act as electrical conduits in opening demonic lynch mob portals that bring increased hatred, division, death and destruction to this earth.

Those who go back to talking to animals, trees, Father Sky and Mother Earth will see the deception, seek to reunify the people and become hunted enemies of the Satanic state.

It's pretty simple. And simplicity is precisely where God can be found.

CHAPTER 20

THE ILLUMINATI 5G END GAME

We are moving rapidly towards what the Illuminati call the New World Order and what David Rockefeller called "The China Model". Rockefeller ought to know since it was he and his Satanic oligarch banker buddies who set up the slave wage corporation we know as modern China.

To understand this model, take a look at the following two articles from Hong Kong's *South China Morning Post* newspaper.

The first written by Stephen Chen on April 29, 2018 is titled, *'Forget the Facebook leak': China is mining data directly from workers' brains on an industrial scale.* In it Chen writes,"Workers outfitted in uniforms staff lines producing sophisticated equipment for telecommunication and other industrial sectors.

But there's one big difference - the workers wear caps to monitor their brainwaves, data that management then uses to adjust the pace of production and redesign workflows, according to the company.

The company said it could increase the overall efficiency of the workers by manipulating the frequency and length of break times to reduce mental stress.

Hangzhou Zhongheng Electric is just one example of the large-scale application of brain surveillance devices to monitor people's emotions and other mental activities in the workplace, according to scientists and companies involved in the government-backed projects.

Concealed in regular safety helmets or uniform hats, these lightweight, wireless sensors constantly monitor the wearer's brainwaves and stream the data to computers that use artificial intelligence algorithms to detect emotional spikes such as depression, anxiety or rage.

The technology is in widespread use around the world but China has applied it on an unprecedented scale in factories, public transport, state-owned companies and the military to increase the competitiveness of its manufacturing industry and to maintain social stability."

Awesome!

The second article, published four days earlier on April 25, 2018 in the *South China Morning Post* was titled, *"Shenzen Police Can Now Identify Drivers Using Facial Recognition Surveillance Cameras"*. Author Li Tao writes,

"Shenzhen is expanding a network of facial recognition surveillance cameras to catch more violations, after the success of an earlier trial to publicly name and shame jaywalkers.

The so-called electronic police system captures photos of vehicles that violate the traffic rules in the metropolis of 12 million people, providing an image of not only the number plate but also the driver's face, which can then be identified from the police database using facial recognition technology. A total of 40 roads will be covered under the expanded surveillance, from the initial single intersection, to identify and fine traffic violators, including those driving without a valid license.

Drivers who had their licenses revoked due to illegal conduct such as driving under the influence of alcohol or drugs have already been captured and identified through the system, according to the Shenzhen Traffic Police's official Sina Weibo account. The system, which went on trial Monday, will be officially launched on May 1.

This move is just the latest in a push by Chinese cities and securities agencies to employ advanced artificial intelligence-based technologies in policing. Earlier this month a fugitive was arrested in southeast China after facial recognition technology helped identify him in a crowd of about 50,000 attending a pop concert. The country is also exporting such technology, with start-up Yitu Technology selling its body mounted cameras equipped with facial recognition software to the Malaysian police.

Traffic violators who are registered with the Shenzhen traffic police - a mandatory step for residents - receive a text message that includes their name, identification card number, and details of the time and location of the offense.

For those who think they are safe from prying electronic eyes under cover of darkness, the new Shenzhen cameras come equipped with night-vision mode."

Double awesome!

China is a Rothschild slave labor laboratory for the Big Brother technology that will gradually be rolled out worldwide. The integrated Orwellian system is known as 5G. And make no mistake, it is a weapon.

In the late 1970's scientists at Lawrence Livermore Laboratories were developing what they called a Brain Bomb - a low-frequency energy weapon that could be used on the battlefield to liquidate the brains of thousands of soldiers at one time.

This weapon was likely used by President George H.W. Bush against Iraqi troops during the 1990 Gulf War, when it was reported that thousands of Iraqi Army troops were simultaneously obliterated near Basra. Their bodies were bulldozed into mass graves and no autopsies were performed.

HAARP (High-Frequency Active Auroral Frequency Program) had already been established in 1933. It was a joint program between the US Air Force, the US Navy, the University of Alaska at Fairbanks and DARPA (Defense Advanced Research Projects Agency).

Based on the stolen research of Nikolas Tesla, HAARP experimented with the weaponization of radio frequencies and energy. Officially it was shut down in 2014, but DARPA carries forward the research, which has now come to focus on the effects of these frequencies on the individual human being.

Currently DARPA - whose logo is a pyramid surrounding the all-seeing eye of the Illuminati - is developing a robotic soldier in tandem with Crown Agent Lockheed Martin.

The Internet was launched and funded by the military as ARPANET in the 1970's. ARPA later became DARPA. On August 6, 1991 the Internet went live to the world and by the end of the 1990's it was being widely used by the public. That was only 20 years ago.

As more people were exposed to DARPA's newest and most widespread low-frequency weapon, school shootings spiked, health problems increased, life-expectancy began a rapid decline, families disintegrated and society began to embrace many dark themes such as vampires and zombies as "normal".

Former DARPA director, Regina Dugan, moved on to Google, where she works with CEO and Bilderberger member Eric Schmidt to promote "smart tattoos", one of which she has herself. It is a bio-metric chip that will be used to access the coming integrated 5G reality that is being rapidly rolled out.

Known as the internet of things, 5G involves hundreds of billions of microchips that will permeate our possessions, our homes, our cars, our neighborhoods and eventually our bodies. Some say that chemtrails are a means by which they are loading our bodies up with aluminum, since this is the best conductor for plugging us into the 5G "smart grid".

In line with the Masonic project that we are nothing more than soul-less batteries to be used to power the Luciferian elite, human beings are slated to become just another "thing" in this Internet of Things. They want to starve us of oxygen and water and change our organic DNA to metal, which they can then mine to run their Babylonian nightmare.

Trans-genderism is an Agenda 21 stepping stone Trojan Horse gateway to trans-humanism, which involves the integration of 5G into our very being. The hip-sounding Silicon Valley front men they are using to promote this Orwellian nightmare are calling it the

Fourth Industrial Revolution. It seeks to integrate smart chip low-frequency weapons technology with biological processes.

The goal is to turn us into machines that can be programmed to perform certain jobs, purchase certain things, think certain thoughts and emit the negative cold dark emotions that will be used to power and normalize the permanent war economy Illuminati blood sacrifice into an acceptable parallel reality they call "virtual reality" or "augmented reality".

Israeli companies are behind this 5G enslavement. They got the Tesla blueprints from James Trump, uncle of President Donald Trump. This explains Trump's moving the US embassy to Jerusalem al-Quds, where the Illuminati Satanists hope to replace the Muslim al Aqsa Mosque with a new version of King Solomon's debaucherous Temple to crown their New World Secular Order.

The violent video games inundating America and destroying our kids are also almost exclusively made by Talmudic Israeli entities in the service of the Crown.

Bitcoin and other crypto-currencies, although portrayed by Max Keiser and other hipster Illuminati shills as some sort of revolt against the private central banking cartel, is actually being rolled out and tested BY the Eight Families Federal Reserve cartel.

A 1992 NSA white paper discussed its viability for use in a cashless society. Indeed it will be the 5G currency that your "tattoo" will store, but only if you are issued "social credit" by the Ministry of Truth. Rebels will get an "access denied" notice from the Beast system.

The Facebook/Cambridge Analytica scandal gave us a glimpse into how Facebook is being used as an emotional dossier gathering tool on each individual for later use by DARPA in their 5G control matrix.

They are mapping everyone's psyche to find out which buttons to push when they hit the 5G switch and transform us all into permanent reliable negative energy batteries for the roll-out and acceptance of their Satanic New World Order.

The divisive 2016 election served to normalize division and reinforced the negative energy environment in which these lower 4th dimension demons operate.

Meanwhile in Switzerland - home to the Bank of International Settlements (BIS), which is the central bank for all the world's private central banks and controls the world via debt slavery - the CERN project continues apace as the Luciferians attempt to isolate the "god particle" using super-high speed atomic fission colliders.

These fallen angel inbreds like to split atoms rather than fuse them since they are all about opposition to a whole Gaia Creation and instead, promote a disjointed atomization of reality that is foreign to this planet. Nuclear fusion could change the world by producing free energy with no waste, but the Satanic bankers wish to take us down the path of nuclear fission, divided reality, conflict with Creator and destruction.

CERN scientists have reported seeing demons during some of their experiments as have other tech "wizards" involved in D-wave quantum computing. They talk about this openly now. One Canadian computer whiz said recently of meeting the demons, "but we still have to push on and hopefully we won't destroy the world in the process."

Some believe CERN is deliberately generating dark matter, that is then funneled into the "cloud", which is Newspeak for the "World Brain" now under construction and set to be completed this year. It will listen, watch, remember and act. A statue of Shiva - Hindu god of destruction - stands at the entrance to CERN headquarters.

This is why the hipster tech leaders talk of "disruptive technology" and "game-changers". Knowingly or not, they are pushing forward this DARPA Luciferian agenda. One company has now created artificial auras for people, while another has produced personal replicas, promoting them as "comforting" in such a suddenly disagreeable world.

Computers have become so powerful that they are now programming themselves. Illuminati spokesman Elon Musk is now warning that unless we want to become these computer's "pets", we must ourselves merge with AI (artificial intelligence). Intel says that by 2020 human brains will contain chips that will run the computers to "prevent" this AI takeover.

These kinds of fear-provoking statements reflect the old Masonic project advancement technique of problem-reaction-solution, or *Ordo Ab Chao* (Order out of Chaos). They first create a problem, then they tell us they can fix it, but only with a Draconian solution that will advance their Great Work of Ages or New World Secular Order.

The Illuminati are obsessed with numbers. They know certain numbers have power. And they do. The ancient spiritual texts all tell us this. Creation is based on a numbers system. But these Luciferians have usurped this ancient knowledge, hidden it from the general populace to keep us dumbed down, and are now using it to enslave us in a Worldwide Web that they have cast out in the hopes of finally capturing the entire human race.

Now enthralled by and willingly caught in their Internet, numbers and algorithms will be key to the coming DARPA endgame called 5G. Once in place it is all math. Human originality, dissent and creativeness are being crushed and discredited as *passe*.

Drones already fly overhead stealing pictures of your face to use as facial recognition software installed in this control matrix. Companies have recently begun asking for a verbal confirmation when you pay bills on the phone. They are stealing your voice, which will then be integrated into the voice recognition software for 5G.

There will be 5G transmitters on every block of every city connecting this "smart grid". Alexa-type devices will monitor every home. Your "smart phone" will track your every purchase, movement, discussion, emotion and thought. It will also implant and change your thoughts and emotions to ones more congruent with the Satanist agenda. Through Facebook, they have learned and will now play upon your weaknesses.

The Hunger Games have begun. And we will all become nothing more than Maze Runners if we do not escape this net of technology that has been cast upon us. When 5G gets rolled out, both our free will and our humanity will be radically curtailed and may cease to exist.

Look around you, it's happening already.

CHAPTER 21

RETURNING TO THE GARDEN OF EDEN

For many, this information may seem overwhelmingly dark, but if we are to heal ourselves and our planet, we must leave our illusions behind and accept what is truly reality.

The Illuminati elite have planted a lie that affects the way we deal with discussing and exposing their own sicknesses. Perception management is their specialty and they want us to perceive that discussing the dark acts they commit is, itself, negative.

In fact, this is a positive act. It is light. When you shine a light on cockroaches, they scatter. Conversely burying our heads in the sand and pretending their atrocities will go away without our active and conscious opposition is what is negative and dark.

The Babylonians use patriarchy to further their agenda of permanent war, depopulation, sexual violence and blood sacrifice. But they also use matriarchy to tamp down dissenters who are told if they talk of these devils, they are being "negative" or wear "tin-foil hats" or whatever other fear-based excuse for docility and inaction they wish to implant in their brains.

We should reject ALL forms of tyranny and inequality. Patriarchy, matriarchy and oligarchy are all forms of "hatriarchy". No being "arches over" any other. This goes against natural law.

These concepts are Luciferian and reflect unbalanced energy in bondage and servitude to a top-down pyramid structure that the Illuminati created. We are all equals. Men, women, blacks, whites, gays, straights, turtles, coyotes, rocks, air, water. We are One.

All that is love is the domain of the God. All that is fear is the domain of Satan. When we expose the heinous actions of these demented Luciferians, we are loving. When we turn our heads away from them, we are fearful and we enable the perpetrators.

There is a scientific term for this mental health condition known as Stockholm Syndrome, where we bow down like cowards to authoritarian figures and cater subconsciously to these oppressors. In doing so, we often betray the very people we love the most.

As Paul Westerberg of The Replacements wrote in the song *Bastards of the Young*, "The ones who love us best are the ones we'll lay to rest, and visit their graves on holidays at best. The ones who love us least are the ones we'll die to please. If it's any consolation, I don't begin to understand it."

The first thing we should do in this epic battle of Good vs. Evil is to learn to flip this brainwashing on its head. When you learn to speak your mind and to stand up to authority, you will also begin to treat those whom you love better. We must all rectify these energy imbalances in our personal lives. Stand up to bullies and energy vampires, while rewarding the decent people in your lives.

Love and truth leads to unity and awareness of the planetary reality that the New Science is proving - that 93% of the universe is energy and only 7% is matter. We are just holograms, our bodies merely shells that contain energy.

The energy we generate scientifically impacts outcomes in the universe. Quantum mechanics is proving that a researcher's vibe affects the experiments being conducted. So it is very important that you wake up every morning and thank Creator for the chance to live another day and to try and do better at sending out good vibes.

Translated into the collective consciousness, we must choose either love of fear. If we choose love, we scientifically unify into one organism and create good healing energy. If we choose fear, we schism into shattered fragments of disjointed negative energy that tears at the very fabric of the cosmos.

Awareness of the enemy and unity of the people are both key to bringing down the dividers of reality - the Babylonians. They seek to fracture all, including the very collective consciousness that is innate to humanity. We must be aware of this and try to get along better with people. Be agreeable where possible.

The Luciferians are disagreeable. This is why they chose to pursue, for example, nuclear fission to create destructive weapons and infinitely toxic waste. Fission is the splitting apart of atoms, the dividing of God's creation.

If they understood creation and wished to accept Creator's Garden of Eden, they would instead pursue nuclear fusion, which seeks to unify atoms to generate unlimited free energy and has no harmful waste as a byproduct.

Energy must be unified, not divided if we wish to live in a healthy, prosperous and scarcity-free world of benefit to all, instead a vampire few.

Unity is the natural order, not chaos, as the trillionaire pedophiles and their minions would have you believe. The New Science Renaissance is debunking the Satanist's age-old "augmented reality" sales pitch that has passed during the many centuries since the so-called Enlightenment for science. But the reality is that even science and religion are One, rather than two disparate concepts. In the end, these crude Illuminati division bell stories were always designed to justify their insatiable rape, pillage and genocide while keeping us off balance.

As the great Indian scholar and revolutionary thinker J. Krishnamurti said, "Truth cannot be realized through any creed, any dogma, any philosophical knowledge, any psychological technique, any ideology, any ritual, or any theological system...you are the world and the world is you. The world is not separate from you and me. There is a common thread of relationship weaving us all together. Deep down we are all connected. Superficially things appear separate. Separate species, separate races, separate cultures and colors, separate nationalities and religions and politics. But if you look closely we are all part of the great tapestry of life. ...When we are ignorant of the fact that all life is interconnected, then we try to control each other...The problem goes much deeper than religion or politics. It starts in our minds, in our habits, in our lives. There is a constant conditioning that has gone on for centuries...We have been conditioned to believe that the observer is separate from the observed, the thinker is separate from the thought.. This dualism, this compartmentalization, is the mother of all conflicts."

This new awareness can transform into good free spirit energy which in turn can unify us in opposition to the very head of the snake - namely the Rothschild-led Illuminati City of London private central banking cartel. If we all continue to pursue single issue fragments of the planetary and cosmic brokenness, it indicates more than anything a misunderstanding of reality.

But if we unite in defense of the whole of Mother Earth and attack the head of the Annunaki serpent together, we can heal the schism in our understanding and thus in the universe. We can then shame the perps, game over, get on with simply living and living simply in this abundant Garden of Eden - and all by lunch time tomorrow.

Simply put the important thing is to become AWARE of the nature of reality. This in turn reveals the gravity and nature of this criminal historical Illuminati assault on our very perception of reality.

Time may be short. Mother Earth is feeling the dis-ease of her inhabitants. We are beyond divided and agitated by all of the methods described in this book.

When you get sick, your body generates a fever to fight the pathogen. In the same way Father Sun is heating up to try and heal the sickness that the Luciferians have wrought upon Mother Earth. Solar flares are increasing, volcanoes and earthquakes are more frequent and the weather is getting more extreme.

Great Spirit is trying to wake us up to tell us that the Seventh Generation is here and that we must rise against the Illuminati and their destruction of Creation. We must do so now because if we do not, the fever may get too high and Earth could die. It is past the time of politics, religion, groups, cliques, isms and division. It is about unity, awareness and revolution - or it is about extinction.

The Luciferians think they have it all figured out, but in the end Creator's patience will run out. As the Australian aborigines - the world's oldest surviving humans - tell us, when that time comes "the sticks and rocks will go in the ground" and it's game over.

The Illuminati and all their ill-gotten wealth will melt into the abyss along with everyone else. A few wise ancients will remain to try and teach the next wave of humans the way of contentment, gratitude, relationship and love in the garden that we have been generously granted.

We've been here before, probably many times, and we'll probably be here again. *Kharma* is scientific. What comes around does go around. A certain action generates an equal and opposite reaction. We can end it all by living according to this axiom.

At some point we will collectively learn to accept our Oneness and to love all life equally. When that point is reached, *dharma* replaces *kharma* and bliss can return to the the Garden of Eden.

These are the darkest of times, but they are also the brightest of times. We must meet the accelerating darkness with an intense and everlasting light based on reality. We must fall back in love with nature and with all of life. It's science.

It's a vision worth fighting for. It's an epic love story. It's the acceptance of a scientific reality which has been there in front of us all along in this Garden of Eden paradise.

"...the wicked know that if the ill they do be of sufficient horror men will not speak against it. That men have just enough stomach for small evils and only these will they oppose. He said that true evil has power to sober the smalldoer against his own deeds and in the contemplation of that evil he may even find the path of righteousness which has been foreign to his feet and have no power but to go upon it. Even this man may be appalled at what is revealed to him and seek some order to stand against it.

Yet in all of this there are two things which perhaps he will not know. He will not know that while the order which the righteous seek is never righteousness itself but is only order, the disorder of evil is in fact the thing itself. Nor will he know that while the righteous are hampered at every turn by their ignorance of evil to the evil all is plain, light and dark alike.

This man of which we speak will seek to impose order and lineage upon things which rightly have none. He will call upon the world itself to testify as to the truth of what are in fact but his desires. In his final incarnation he may seek to indemnify his words with blood for by now he will have discovered that words pale and lose their savor while pain is always anew".

Cormac McCarthy, "The Crossing"

ABOUT THE AUTHOR

Dean Henderson was born in Faulkton, South Dakota. He earned a BLS at the University of South Dakota and an M.S. in Environmental Studies from the University of Montana, where he edited *The Missoula Paper* and was a columnist for the *Montana Kaimin*. His articles have appeared in *Multinational Monitor, In These Times, Paranoia* and hundreds of online websites and magazines.

A life-long activist and traveler to 50 countries, Henderson appears regularly as a political analyst for Iran's Press TV, RT, Russian Channel 1, The Syria Times, Rense Radio,Tactical Talk with Zain Khan and The Richie Allen Show. In June 2018, Dean spoke at New York City's Deep Truth conference where he delivered a speech titled, "All Roads Lead to the City of London" as part of a panel named Confronting Oligarchy: Resisting Full Spectrum Dominance.

Dean and his wife Jill live in the Missouri Ozarks where the rivers run clear, the water tastes sweet and the air is clean. They operate and live on a small organic vegetable farm, burn wood for heat, and gather wild berries, mushrooms, fruits and nuts. They don't work slave wage jobs and buy very little, living a simple and rich life.

Subscribe free to Dean's weekly column and interviews at
HendersonLeftHook.wordpress.com

Left Hook

by Dean Henderson

MORE BOOKS BY DEAN HENDERSON

Big Oil & Their Bankers in the Persian Gulf
Four Horsemen, Eight Families & Their Global Narcotics & Terror Network

An internationally acclaimed best-seller that started the recent conversation about who really runs the world, Big Oil... exposes a centuries-old cabal of global oligarchs that control the global economy through manipulation of the world's central banks via the planet's three most valuable commodities: oil, guns and drugs.

Stickin' It to the Matrix

Stickin' it to the Matrix is this generation's version of Abbie Hoffman's Steal This Book. Funny and irreverent, it is above all a practical step-by-step guide to both escaping and extracting from the matrix. In Stickin' it to the Matrix, Henderson offers the reader the same insights that allowed him to "retire" at age 28, move to the country and author this and other books.

The Federal Reserve Cartel

The Federal Reserve Cartel is a brief, well-documented history of the Eight Families who control the world's private central banks and most of the planet's resources.

The Grateful Unrich
Revolution in 50 Countries

Covering fifty countries on six continents over a twenty-year span, Henderson asks the hard social, political and economic questions while vagabonding his way around the world. Invoking the wit and humor of Twain and the curiosity of Kerouac, Henderson discovers himself, humanity and revolutionary politics through prolonged contact with God's chosen people - The Grateful Unrich.

Nephilim Crown 5G Apocalypse

Nephilim Crown 5G Apocalypse is an indictment of the computer revolution as the latest mechanism through which royal bloodline families seek to control humanity. The roll out of their battlefield 5G weapons system represents the pinnacle in their use of electromagnetic frequencies to literally remote control their human herd. Since their intervention in Sumeria, these hybrid fallen angel Nephilim have usurped, steered, and plundered all of Creation as self-appointed god kings. The coming 5G apocalypse represents a great unveiling of not only their nefarious 5G deception, but of the fraudulent Nephilim Crown itself.

ABOUT THE AUTHOR

Jill Henderson is an author, artist and backwoods herbalist with a passion for wild edible medicinal plants and culinary herbs. A featured columnist for *Acres USA* and longtime contributor to *Llewellyn's Herbal Almanac,* Jill's articles have been featured online and in print magazines such as the *Permaculture Activist, Permaculture Design,* and *The Essential Herbal.*

For more than 25 years, Jill has been an organic gardener, seed saver, and passionate advocate for sustainable agriculture. She often writes about the global challenges presented by GMOs and teaches gardeners and small farmers how to avoid them by saving their own open-pollinated and heirloom seeds.

In addition to her books, Jill is the author and editor of Show Me Oz, a weekly blog filled with in-depth articles on gardening, seed saving, homesteading, wildcrafting, edible and medicinal plants, herbs, nature, and more. She also sells her unique artwork at ForeverPetPortraits.wordpress.com.

Jill and her husband Dean live in the heart of the rugged Missouri Ozarks, where they grow and wildcraft a wide array of organic herbs, fruits, and vegetables on their rural homestead with their furry feline, Loris.

Connect with Jill at
ShowMeOz.wordpress.com

SHOW ME
OZ
. W O R D P R E S S . C O M

MORE BOOKS BY JILL HENDERSON

The Healing Power of Kitchen Herbs
Growing and Using Nature's Remedies

A no-nonsense guide that is literally jam-packed with proven information on growing, harvesting and using the world's safest and most flavorful culinary herbs to spice up your favorite dish, beautify the landscape, attract beneficial insects, and create safe and effective natural healing herbal remedies at home.

A Journey of Seasons
A Year in the Ozarks High Country

Take a walk through the Ozark highlands with herbalist, naturalist, and armadillo whisperer, Jill Henderson, as she takes you through the changing landscapes of the seasons. This delightfully inspiring book is filled with nature notes, botanical musings, backwoods wisdom, and just a pinch of "hillbilly" humor. This is one journey you don't want to miss!

The Garden Seed Saving Guide
Easy Heirloom Seeds for the Home Gardener

As the world food and seed supply is being been hijacked by powerful corporate interests, saving seeds is a skill that everyone needs to learn to survive. Praised by gardeners and seed savers alike, this little no-nonsense book will teach you everything you need to know to start saving your own organic seeds in less than 50 pages.

Made in the USA
San Bernardino, CA
03 January 2020